The Staffordshire Regiments

"KNOTTED TOGETHER"

The Imperial, Regular
and Volunteer Regiments 1705-1919

Dave Cooper

To Val
Best Wishes
Dave Cooper
11th December 2003

Acknowledgements

A book of this type cannot be written without the help of the many people and organisations who have assisted and encouraged me throughout the research and compilation. Most important amongst these are Carole, my wife, and Matthew, Jessica and Nicholas my children, whose patience has known no bounds; my Mother who has proof-read hundreds of A4 sheets on various unfamiliar Staffordshire regiments for hours on end and helped in compiling the text, and my Father who has taken the many digital photographs for the illustrations.

I am also indebted to Mrs Irene Moore of *The Armourer* magazine whose foresight, enthusiasm and encouragement persuaded me to commence my initial article covering my collecting interest in the Imperial Volunteer and Regular Regiments of Staffordshire.

I am indebted to Brig. S.J. Knapper CBE MC Col, The Staffordshire Regiment (The Prince of Wales's), Lt-Colonel A.J Scott (retd) MBE, Major P. Mulingani, Mrs A S Elsom (Curator) and all the other staff at the Staffordshire Regimental Museum, Whittington Barracks near Lichfield. A visit there is strongly advised.

Grateful thanks are extended to Lt-Colonel D. German, TD, DL, JP, and the Trustees of The Staffordshire Yeomanry (Queen's Own Royal Regiment), Ancient High House, Stafford for their help. Again, a visit is highly recommended.

I wish also to acknowledge Maurice Holland for access to his exhaustive files on the Staffordshire Yeomanry, and for his help with the First Staffordshire Volunteer Artillery; and the assistance and advice of the seasoned authors Peter Lead, Chris Coogan, Andy Thornton, Jake Whitehouse and Jeff Elson. Thanks also to Terry Reece, Chris Ecclestone, Wally Johnson and the late Mr Eric Owen, who have all contributed, sometimes unwittingly, with large amount, or just mere snippets, of information and advice.

My thanks also to my many friends and colleagues in this country and abroad, fellow dealers, collectors, re-enactors, modellers, restoration or research enthusiasts, who have spoken well of my articles in *The Armourer.* By so doing they have been instrumental in the completion of this book.

Amongst the illustrations for this book are a collection of authentic representations of soldiers of early Staffordshire regiments by Rob Chapman of Flintlock Publishing. These were reproduced in full colour in *The Armourer* with my original articles. Flintlock Publishing produce American War of Independence, French and Indian Wars and other military paintings, in cards and prints.

They are available from: Flintlock Publishing,
Old Furnace Cottage, Greendale, Oakamoor, Staffs, ST10 3AP.
01538 703860   email: RobPics@aol.com Web: www.robchapman.biz

All weaponry displayedin this book has been deactivated or is inert.

CHURNET VALLEY BOOKS
6 Stanley Street, Leek, Staffordshire. ST13 5HG 01538 399033
thebookshopleek.co.uk
© David Cooper and Churnet Valley Books 2003
ISBN 1 904546 03 X

Contents

Foreword

Dave Cooper's interesting and fact-filled book chronicles the history of Staffordshire soldiers over the past 400 years. Many of the chapters appeared originally in *The Armourer* magazine, where I know they have given great pleasure and have proved a useful source of reference. These articles have been collected together, collated and expanded to provide a continuous story, the copious illustrations often from Dave Cooper's own extensive collection.

Dave has been a strong supporter of The Staffordshire Regiment Museum for a number of years and, of course, has had access to our regimental archive. He has combined the history of The Staffordshire Regiment with other military organisations that have been based in, or recruited from, the County, and although primarily a military book, it will be of interest to any student of the history of the County.

The book fills a significant gap, since the histories of both North and South Staffordshire Regiments are out of print, whilst that of their successor, The Staffordshire Regiment, is only now being written and will not be available for several years. Interest in military history has never been higher and there is great curiosity throughout the County about the careers of fathers, grandfathers and other relatives who, in peace or war, served in the Army. Dave has answered the need in generous measure; he has sensibly avoided too deep a work but has highlighted all the essentials and provided a liberal sprinkling of detail to flesh out his story.

As Colonel of The Staffordshire Regiment, I welcome this new telling of our history and that of all Staffordshire soldiers, whatever their cap-badge. I am sure this book will be of great value.

Brigadier Simon Knapper CBE, MC.

Preface

I became fascinated with all aspects of military history, research and acquisition over 30 years ago, in particular in the county of Staffordshire, especially the Imperial Regiments up until the end of the Great War, and to a lesser extent the English Civil War within Staffordshire. I was continually disappointed that there was not a detailed book on all the volunteer and regular regiments who have served in and from Staffordshire. With a few notable exceptions, very little had been printed on the Staffordshire Militia, the Staffordshire Rifle or Artillery Volunteers.

It is common knowledge within military collectors and researchers, in Great Britain and around the globe, that the regular Staffordshire regiments served all over the world, taking part in nearly every war and battle in which British forces were engaged for 300 years. Such people will be familiar with the numbered, and later County regiments, the North Staffordshire (The Prince of Wales's) or South Staffordshire Regiment.

It is a matter of fact that the Staffordshire's regular battalions were seldom in Staffordshire at all. They disappeared for years on end, constantly shifting station, employed in some corner of the world "propping up the Empire". Staffordshire men and women can be proud that it was with the blood and bones of Staffordshire men that the British Empire was built; there is not an ocean or continent in which Staffordshire men do not rest as silent memorials. Sir John Fortescue, a famous Army historian, once said of the South Staffords: "one could not help reflecting that if this regiment wore the kilt, the whole British Army would ring with its fame".

But there were also county militia, rifle volunteers, yeomanry cavalry and volunteer artillery who were very active within Staffordshire, and indeed the rest of Great Britain, and in some instances even abroad on active service. These volunteer regiments were very much in evidence in the Victorian era, part-time soldiers serving their Queen and Country.

I was induced to write this book because I wished to record the hitherto lesser known histories of the various Staffordshire militia, yeomanry, rifle and artillery volunteer regiments, who with the exception of the militia, were later absorbed into the Territorials. The most famous of these was the 137th Staffordshire Brigade, who served with the 46th North Midland (Territorial Force) Division during the Great War with such distinction.

The Staffordshire Militia and the Volunteer Battalions became the 3rd and 4th Battalions of the South Staffordshire and the North Staffordshire Regiments, belonging to the Special Reserve from 1908. At the end of the 1914-18 War these Special Reserve battalions did not reform (though they are still shown in Army Lists) . After nearly 300 years of faithful, if broken and unspectacular service, like all good old soldiers, they just faded away!

Over seven years of research and compilation have gone into *Knotted Together*. I do not consider myself an expert, only a knowledgeable student, and it is certain that I have not got everything right. I wish to encourage the emergence of new facts and artifacts. Indeed, information and artifacts could well reside in the private collection of a reader of this book, unaware that it is a previously unrecorded item, and I hope that if this is the case the custodian will make known the item, anonymously if so desired, so that details can be made available to researchers and collectors.

This book is a long way from being the last word on the Imperial and Volunteer Regiments of Staffordshire, but I have tried hard to achieve a readable and interesting work that is accurate and comprehensive.

DAVE COOPER, Stoke-on-Trent, Staffordshire.

The Staffordshire Volunteers

STAFFORDSHIRE RIFLE VOLUNTEERS

Formation of Corps (see footnote for details and numbering) and subsequent organisation into Administrative Battalions

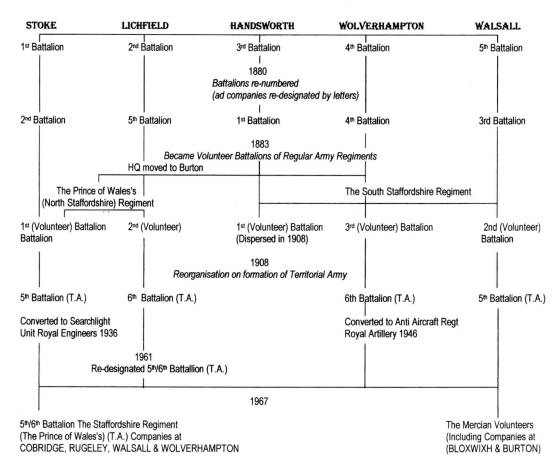

STOKE	LICHFIELD	HANDSWORTH	WOLVERHAMPTON	WALSALL
1st Battalion	2nd Battalion	3rd Battalion	4th Battalion	5th Battalion

1880
Battalions re-numbered
(ad companies re-designated by letters)

STOKE	LICHFIELD	HANDSWORTH	WOLVERHAMPTON	WALSALL
2nd Battalion	5th Battalion	1st Battalion	4th Battalion	3rd Battalion

1883
Became Volunteer Battalions of Regular Army Regiments
HQ moved to Burton

The Prince of Wales's
(North Staffordshire) Regiment   The South Staffordshire Regiment

1st (Volunteer) Battalion Battalion	2nd (Volunteer)	1st (Volunteer) Battalion (Dispersed in 1908)	3rd (Volunteer) Battalion	2nd (Volunteer) Battalion

1908
Reorganisation on formation of Territorial Army

5th Battalion (T.A.)	6th Battalion (T.A.)		6th Battalion (T.A.)	5th Battalion (T.A.)
Converted to Searchlight Unit Royal Engineers 1936			Converted to Anti Aircraft Regt Royal Artillery 1946	

1961
Re-designated 5th/6th Battallion (T.A.)

1967

5th/6th Battalion The Staffordshire Regiment
(The Prince of Wales's) (T.A.) Companies at
COBRIDGE, RUGELEY, WALSALL & WOLVERHAMPTON

The Mercian Volunteers
(Including Companies at
(BLOXWIXH & BURTON)

NOTE

During the formation years 1859-1860 the following Corps were in existence and were incorporated into Administrative Battalions as shown. The Corps were originally numbered and changed to the lettered companies in the reorganisation of 1880.

STOKE BATTALION	LICHFIELD/BURTON BATTALION	HANDSWORTH BATTALION	WOLVERHAMPTON BATTALION	WALSALL BATTALION
2nd (A) LONGTON	7th (A) BURTON	1st (A & B) HANDSWORTH	5th (A, B & C) WOLVERHAMPTON	4th (A & B) WALSALL
3rd (B) HANLEY	8th (B) BURTON	15th (C) BRIERLEY HILL	11th (E) TIPTON	14th (C) BLOXWICH
6th (C) BURSLEM	19th (C) TAMWORTH	17th SEISDON	12th (G & H) BILSTON	33rd (E) CANNOCK
10th (E) STOKE	24th (E) LICHFIELD	20th (E) WEST BROMWICH	26th (D) WILLENHALL	34th (F) WEDNESBURY
13th (F) KIDSGROVE	25th F & G) STAFFORD	(F) SUTTON COLDFIELD	29th (F) SEDGLEY	
16th (G & H) NEWCASTLE	39th (H) BURTON	27th (G) PATSHULL	30th (M) TETTENHALL	
28th (I) LEEK		31st (M) SMETHWICK	32nd (K & I) WOLVERHAMPTON	
36th (K) HANLAY		35th KINVER		
37th CHEADLE				
38th ECCLESHALL				
40th (L) STONE				

Courtesy of the Right Hon. Bruce George M.P.

One
Origins of the Stafford Knot and the Staffordshire Militia

Intertwined cords in the form of a slackened knot make a particularly good badge, and a very useful rallying point during a battle. The Stafford knot displayed on all regimental devices of the various Staffordshire regiments is unique and very easy to recognise. It was the heraldic symbol of the ancient Norman Barons de Stafford, who were later to become the Earls of Stafford, and also the Dukes of Buckingham. The first was a companion to William the Conqueror in 1066.

This knot is now ever present in heraldic devices in Staffordshire and is generally referred to as a 'Staffordshire' knot. Other, similar, heraldic knots were used by families such as Heneage, Lacy, Bourchier, Bowen and Harrington on their standards, armour and shields.

The Staffordshire Militia

As long ago as Saxon times, it was compulsory for all able-bodied men to serve in the 'Fyrd' or militia, which gradually developed into the British Army.

The large landowners raised the Militia, each county having to provide their own quota when called upon. The Militia at that time were known as 'Trained Bands'. No standing army existed in those days in the British Isles. This meant that these "Trained Bands" disbanded as soon as the need, such as invasions and other warlike disturbances, had passed.

The Royalist and Parliamentary forces were the first armies, displaying the characteristics of standing armies during the English Civil War. But the first permanent standing army was created by Charles II who enrolled General Monk's Regiment, the Coldstream, and another regiment from Dunkirk, along with two other regiments of foot.

Following the statute of 1662, the appointment of officers, disposal of arms and command of the 'Trained Bands' took place, and for the first time in the history of the British Army, the 'Trained Bands' were called militia.

Prior to the formation of Staffordshire's Regular Foot Regiments, Staffordshire's Militia can be traced back to 1648, when Colonel John Bowyer of Knypersley, close to Stoke-on-Trent, commanded a regiment of foot and two troops of horse.

It is known that several other "White Coat" Regiments and troops of horse were also raised, one by Colonel Bagot of Blithfield near Uttoxeter. They fought for the Royalist cause during the English Civil War, and also garrisoned the then moated and curtain walled Lichfield Cathedral. This was one of the final Royalist garrisons to surrender, on the orders of Charles I who by then was virtually a prisoner of the Scottish army. His capital in exile, Oxford, fell on 26th June 1646, and the Lichfield garrison only marched out to surrender on 16th July, when any chance of raising the siege had finally disappeared.

That Bonnie Prince Charlie marched into England (and coincidentally through the Staffordshire Moorlands, fighting a skirmish with King George's Dragoons in the village of Ipstones on his way to Derby in the 1745 rebellion), with a few thousand men virtually unopposed, illustrates the incompetence and pathetic state of the Militia force in general, who, at this time, had hardly even been called out for drill in five years, let alone seen active service.

The year 1793 saw the outbreak of war with Napoleonic France, and the Militia en Masse was embodied. Staffordshire provided 600 men, their colonel being Lord Paget. The Pagets later went on to become the Marquises of Anglesey following the Napoleonic Wars.

The Staffordshire Volunteers

With only the roughest and poorest men, who could not afford to pay for a substitute, serving in the compulsory Militia, the Militia was perceived as a rabble. Only the very real threat of invasion spurred any volunteers to join them at all. This was realised by Parliament with its Volunteer Act of 1794.

Infantry officer's spadroon sword, with a maker's date on it of 1794. The 'Cigar Band' is engraved with King George III's crown over 'L.S.V.' (Loyal Stafford Volunteers) surmounting an engraved Stafford Knot.

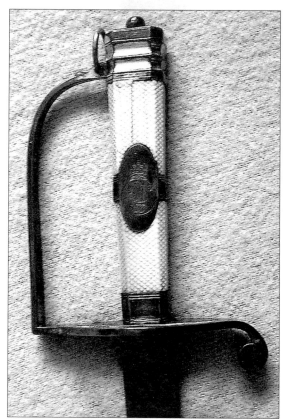

In 1794, in the country as a whole, Volunteers (known as Loyal Volunteers) were formed, including the Loyal Stafford Volunteers, though still being attached as extra companies to the Militia. 1798 saw the emergence of a separate Volunteer Force (called Armed Associations), the idea being for these troops to stay within their local parishes, and to harass and snipe enemy troops, (similar to the British Home Guard of the Second World War), rather than to fight in pitched battles.

Following the short lived peace of Amiens) signed on the 27th March 1802, 1803 saw the re-start of hostilities and a form of conscription under the Levy En Masse Act. Here, of the 500,000 eligible males aged 17-55 in the country, fully 463,000 had volunteered by the end of the year. In contrast to the Armed Associations, these Volunteers were subject to the Mutiny Act, had to agree to serve anywhere in the kingdom, and to fight against an enemy or to suppress rebellious fellow Englishmen.

The Local Militia Act of 1808, produced 200,000 18-33 year olds by ballot. Unlike before, these could not be substituted and serving Volunteers had to transfer into the Militia. With the defeat of Napoleon at Waterloo in 1815 and the end of the war, the Local Militia Act was suspended in 1816, and many Volunteers then disbanded.

In 1807, a 77 mm, hallmarked, silver medal was presented to a member of Stone Volunteers, for *"Ball firing, a reward for skill from Major R. W. Topp September 1807"*.

EXTRACT FROM THE REGIMENTAL ORDER BOOK

OF THE

Hanley and Shelton Volunteer Infantry,

4th JUNE, 1808.

The Battalion to parade tomorrow morning with Side Arms for Church at ½ past 6 oclock

The Serjeant Major Simpkin will direct a record to be made in this Order Book of the transactions of this day in order that the important transactions of it may be referred to and be perpetuated to a period of time when we shall be no longer Soldiers.

The non commissioned Officers and Privates of this Battalion being anxious to testify by some public marks of approbation the high sense they entertain of the unremitting attention of Colonel Whitehead to the interests of the Corps, from the period of its being embodied, unanimously determined to purchase a sword of the value of £30 and to present it to him during their stay upon permanent duty at Ashbourne. Agreeably to the resolution after the Battalion had returned to the Town from its morning Exercise on the 4th of June, and while it was drawn up in the Street for the purpose of firing a feu Joilee in honour of their Sovereigns Birthday, the Serjeant Major accompanied by the other Serjeants in the centre of the Line and in the presence of an immense crowd of spectators, presented the sword to the Colonel with the following address.

Colonel Whitehead I am deputed by the non

commissioned Officers and Privates to present you with this Sword as a proof of their sincere attachment. We consider ourselves happy in this opportunity of offering a public testimony of our approbation of your very meritorious conduct since the formation of this Battalion and we heartily wish that you may live long to wear it in defence of our King and Country.

As soon as the Colonel had delivered up his own and received the Sword from the Serjeant Major he addressed the Battalion in the following Terms.

Answer

After the experience of nearly six years there needed not the proof of your attachment to me the recollection of it on my mind has long since secured all my exertions for the honor of the Battalion and has very amply rewarded me for the trouble which my military duties have imposed upon me. I accept this proof of your esteem with sentiments of the greatest respect. I hope I may consider it as a token of your liberty to the cause in which we are engaged and should our more active services be ever required in defence of our King and Country then this Sword must be our rallying point.

It is thought expedient to record in the Orderly Book this transaction which is so honorable to all the parties concerned, for the double purpose of exhibiting a noble instance of generosity in the Men who volunteered their gratuitous services in defence of their King and Country as well as of evincing to Officers generally but particularly to those of this Battalion, that attention to discipline is sure to command from a British Soldier correspondent returns of gratitude and attachment.

"Extract from the Regimental Order Book of the Hanley and Shelton Volunteer Infantry, 4th June 1808."

Officers' mess china plate, 2nd King's Own
Stafford Militia c. 1800

King's Own Stafford Militia helmet plate from an
Albert pattern shako 1844-1855

Staffordshire Rifle Volunteers tunic
top circa 1860.

It was not until 1858, with increasing animosity
between the old enemies of France and Britain, that
Volunteers were again proposed by the British
Government. The County Lord Lieutenants
commissioned officers and organised oaths
of allegiance and call-out. In the time of
call-out, Volunteers were subject to
military law, but also had to receive pay
like their regular counterparts. All
Volunteers were exempt from the
Militia Ballot, but had to perform
drill daily for eight days in every
four months. A fortnight's notice
of resignation was also required.

Though some finances to
form and equip Volunteers
were obtained from public
subscriptions, Volunteers were
often expected to provide their
own uniforms, arms and
equipment. This may help to
explain why this Staffordshire
Rifle Volunteers tunic top,
and shako plates, circa 1860,
have managed to survive the
ravages of time.

Staffordshire Rifle Volunteers
shako plate circa 1860.

Staffordshire Militia shako plate
circa 1860.

In 1861 government arms were issued to the full compliment of the 40 Volunteer Corps in the county, along with free ammunition. Annual camps were established in Aldershot and Shorncliffe. These ranked in precedence according to their dates of formation, with Handsworth ranking No. 1, and Stone ranking No. 40. However Staffordshire Volunteer Artillery (such as the Shelton Battery) still ranked senior to the Rifle Volunteers.

The 1862 Royal Commission recommended that every Rifle Volunteer attend nine drills a year, six of which were to be battalion parades, to obtain a £1 subsidy grant. A further 10s was available to every volunteer who had fired 60 rounds, passing as a 3rd class shot.

The interest was so unexpectedly great, that these 40 corps formed five Admin. Battalions, No. 1 being Stoke, No. 2 Lichfield in the south of the county; No. 3 Handsworth; No. 4 Wolverhampton and No. 5 Walsall, all of the last three now in the West Midlands and no longer Staffordshire.

By 1872 the Kinver and Eccleshall - Staffordshire Rifle Volunteers had disbanded, but 1873 saw a further revival of interest up until the introduction of new Regulations in 1886.

The 1881 complete re-organisation saw the previously numbered

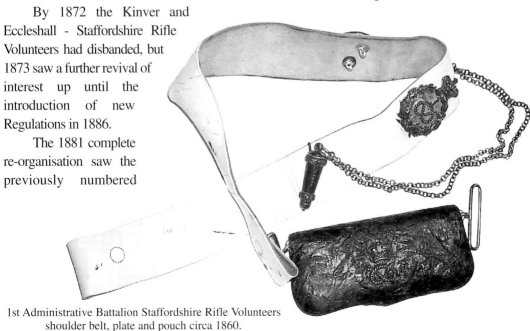

1st Administrative Battalion Staffordshire Rifle Volunteers
shoulder belt, plate and pouch circa 1860.

regiments, the 38th (1st Staffordshire) and the 80th (Staffordshire Volunteers - originally created from Volunteers of the Staffordshire Militia) transform into the 1st and 2nd Battalions respectively of the South Staffordshire Regiment. Similarly the previously numbered 64th (2nd Staffordshire) and 98th (with no previous Staffordshire attachment), transformed into the 1st and 2nd Battalions respectively of the North Staffordshire Regiment.

Two militia battalions attached to each of these new regiments became the 3rd and 4th Battalions of each, along with volunteer battalions attached to the Regular Regiment, in the case of the South Staffordshire Regiment, the 1st, 2nd and 3rd Volunteer Battalions, and for the North Staffordshire Regiment, the 1st and 2nd Volunteer Battalions .

During the Boer War, Imperial Yeomanry, including the Staffordshire Yeomanry, offered and had their services accepted, as did the Volunteers, into active service companies attached to county regiments.

The Territorial and Reserve Forces Act of 1907 changed second line forces. The 23 Militias disbanded all together. The rest changed into the Special Reserve. The 1 V.B. and 2 V.B. South Staffordshire Regiment became the 5th Battalion South Staffordshire Regiment in 1908. The 3rd V.B. of the South Staffordshire Regiment also became the 6th Bn South Staffordshire Regiment in 1908. The 1st V.B. and 2nd V.B.s of the North Staffordshire Regiment became the 5th Battalion and 6th Battalion respectively of the North Staffordshire Regiment in 1908.

This may explain why this 3rd Volunteer Battalion South Staffordshire Regiment shoulder belt and pouch had been painted with gold paint when first acquired, presumably in 1908 at the time of these changes. It is now restored to its original silver glory.

An interesting footnote - the Leek Corp of the 1st V.B. North Staffordshire Regiment became a corps of the Staffordshire Volunteer Artillery in 1807, fighting throughout the First World War in the 46th North Midland, Territorial Force, Royal Artillery.

THE STAFFORDSHIRE MILITIA

Prior to Staffordshire's Regular Foot Regiments, its Militia can be traced back to the 1640s. The Royalist and Parliamentarian forces 1642-1652 were the first armies to display the characteristics of standing armies, in the English Civil War, and, within Staffordshire, Colonel Bagot raised a regiment of foot and troops of horse. A regiment of irregulars were also commanded around the Leek area by Colonel Watson. In 1648 Colonel John Bowyer of Knypersley commanded a regiment of foot and two troops of horse.

Following the statute of 1662, the appointment of officers, disposal of arms and command of the trained bands took place, and for the first time trained bands were called militia.

Since 1662 there are records of militias being embodied, including in the years 1776-1785, 1793-1801, 1805-1814 and 1815-1816. In 1805 King George III conferred on the 1st Staffordshire Regiment of Militia, the title King's Own Staffordshire Militia. From 1816 the Militia was in abeyance until 1852.

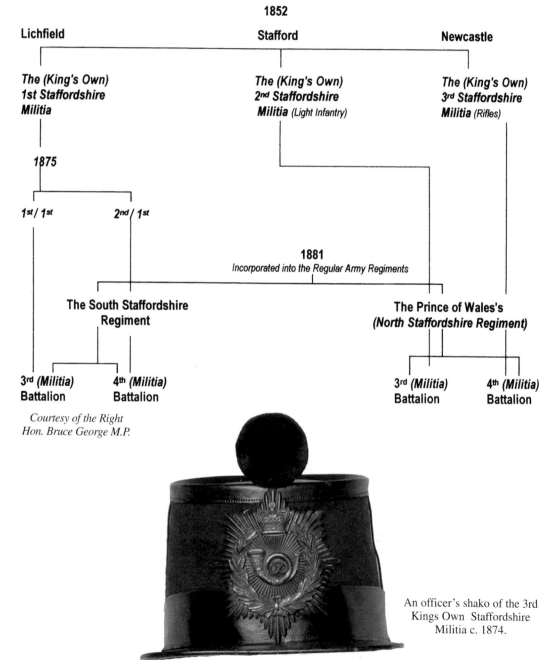

1852

Lichfield	Stafford	Newcastle
The (King's Own) 1st Staffordshire Militia	The (King's Own) 2nd Staffordshire Militia (Light Infantry)	The (King's Own) 3rd Staffordshire Militia (Rifles)

1875

1st / 1st   2nd / 1st

1881
Incorporated into the Regular Army Regiments

The South Staffordshire Regiment

The Prince of Wales's (North Staffordshire Regiment)

3rd (Militia) Battalion   4th (Militia) Battalion

3rd (Militia) Battalion   4th (Militia) Battalion

Courtesy of the Right Hon. Bruce George M.P.

An officer's shako of the 3rd Kings Own Staffordshire Militia c. 1874.

Shoulder belt plates 5th Staffordshire Rifle Volunteers, Glengarry badge and waist belt clasp.

A Boer War Tribute group of medals to Pte J Rowbotham, F company of
the 2nd V.B. of the North Staffordshire Regiment from Stafford.

Two
The Raising of the Staffordshire Yeomanry Cavalry and a Brief History to the End of the First World War

With the breakout of the Napoleonic wars, Parliament empowered counties to raise Volunteer Yeomanry Cavalry in 1793. The magistrates and Lieutenants of Staffordshire organised the subscriptions for buying the arms and uniforms with which to equip the Staffordshire Volunteer Cavalry, or the Staffordshire Regiment of Gentlemen and Yeomanry, who were formed at a County Committee meeting in the Swan Hotel, Stafford - still a hotel 200 years later .

The motto "Pro Aris et Focis" (for our hearths and our homes) and the Stafford Knot were adopted, along with a scarlet uniform with yellow facings. The Regiment initially comprised five divisions. The Leek Division was commanded by Captain James Bulkeley. The Regimental Colonel was Earl Gower of the Newcastle Division. The Stafford Division was commanded by Lt. Colonel, the Hon. Monckton. The other two divisions were the Lichfield and Walsall Divisions commanded by Major F. P. Elliot and Captain William Tennant respectively.

However these were by no means the only cavalry in Staffordshire. 'Armed Associations' in other parts of the county formed their own troops of cavalry, including the Loyal Bilston Troop, Wolverhampton, Tamworth and Royal Pottery Troop, being accepted in 1798. Two other troops were also being raised - the Needwood Troop of Volunteer Cavalry and the Stone and Eccleshall Volunteer Cavalry.

The Queen's Own Royal Staffordshire Yeomanry
Troops and Squadrons 1794 - 1906

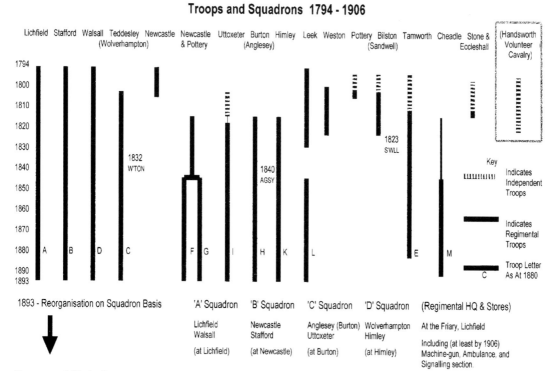

Courtesy of Chris Coogan.

A Georgian crowned
Staffordshire Yeomanry
officer's pouch and belt,
early 18th century.

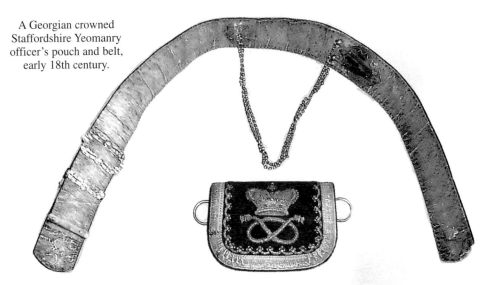

During its entire thirty year existence, the Loyal Handsworth Volunteer Cavalry was independent from the Staffordshire Yeomanry. In October 1800 the Sixth Weston Troop was added by Lord Bradford. Wolverhampton Armed Association and the Needwood Troop disbanded after the 1802 treaty, but with 1803's resumption of the war all six Yeomanry and the four independent troops continued their service.

The Bagots of Blithfield raised the Uttoxeter Cavalry via Captain, the Honourable Claud Bagot. In the same year the Teddersley troop, raised by Captain Moreton Walhouse of Wolverhampton, became the seventh troop. Again in 1803, Captain Simpson's Pottery Association Cavalry became the eighth troop of the Regiment, and in June 1805, The Loyal Bilston Association joined the Regiment.

1813's Army Regulations required amalgamations into larger troops, and although the Loyal Handsworth remained independent, the Uttoxeter, Tamworth and Stone and Eccleshall troops all joined the growing Regiment. However, with the intervention of peace in the spring of 1814, the Stone and Eccleshall troop disbanded along with the majority of the Uttoxeter Troop, though a few of the Uttoxeter Yeomen transferred into the Lichfield Troop, and the whole of the Tamworth Troop now joined the Regiment.

1827 saw the last remaining independent troop in the county, the Loyal Handsworth Volunteer Cavalry, disbanded as a result of Government regulations of that year.

In October 1835 the Regiment was presented by the Duchess of Sutherland, the Countess of Lichfield, the Countess of Dartmouth, Lady Hatherton and Lady Peel with five squadron guidons (standards). One was red, the other four were of white silk, bearing the Stafford Knot enclosed by a garter with the Regimental motto and surmounted by a Royal crown.

Queen Victoria was crowned in 1838, and in commemoration of the escort provided by the Regiment on her visit to Shugborough in 1832, one of her first acts was to bestow a Royal title upon the Regiment, The Queen's Royal Regiment of Staffordshire Yeomanry Cavalry.

With the fringes of Birmingham to the south, and Stoke-on-Trent (the Potteries) to the North, the Staffordshire Yeomanry was one of the busiest Victorian 'anti-riot squads' of all yeomanry regiments nationwide.

The Moorlands Squadron was established in December 1842 by influential inhabitants in the

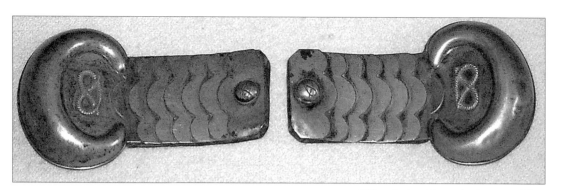

Officer's shoulder scales buttons of the Queen's Royal Regiment of Staffordshire Yeomanry Cavalry which just comprised of a Staffordshire Knot - so predating 1838.

Officer's epaulettes of the Queen's Own Royal Regiment with QORR on the epaulette buttons as well as the Staffordshire Knot, making them post 1838.

Centre section of one of the October 1835 colours presented by the Duchess of Sutherland and others, as described in text.

An officer's bell top shako of the Staffordshire Yeomanry Cavalry, circa 1829-1844

The obverse and reverse of a Queen's Own Royal Yeomanry medal in silver, the obverse with the Staffordshire Knot surmounted by the Queen's Crown. The reverse centre states FIRM AND CONSTANT, surrounded by an acorn wreath, at the top PRIVATE WILLIAM WARD, and at the bottom the date 1840

North East of the County and was based at Leek and Cheadle. The following year a guidon was presented to the Moorland troop at Uttoxeter by the Earl of Shrewsbury, very similar in pattern to the ones presented previously in 1835.

A Staffordshire Yeomanry bandsman's sword - very similar to the 6th Dragoon Guards bandsman's sword.

Colonel Bromley-Davenport's Albert Pattern helmet, with post 1860's white plume - prior to this the plume would have been black.

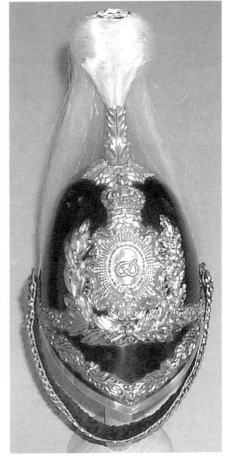

1861 was the first year a competition for musketry was held in the place of swordsmanship, and 480 Westly Richards percussion carbines were released to the Regiment in 1870. The Regiment continued to be one of the strongest recruited Yeomanry Regiments.

At the 1881 annual training 477 Yeoman including eighteen bandsmen of an enrolled strength of 466 were recorded as present. Snider carbines were issued, and a cup given by the officers for an annual shooting competition.

Following the death of Colonel Bromley-Davenport during the 1884 training, Major and the Hon. Lt-

A Staffordshire Yeomanry sabretache c.1875, formerly the property of the Earl of Shrewsbury.

Colonel, the Marquis of Anglesey, was promoted to command the Regiment. The following year, 1885, saw the issue of Martini Henry carbines.

The Cheadle troop disbanded in 1892, the new establishment being 488 of all rank in nine troops as follows: A - Lichfield; B - Stafford; C - Wolverhampton; D - Walsall; E - 1st Newcastle; F - 2nd Newcastle; G - Anglesey (as the Burton-on-Trent troop had been known since 1840); H - Uttoxeter, and I - Himley.

The Yeomanry re-organisation of 1893 saw the Staffordshire Yeomanry brigaded (like their regular counterparts) with the Warwickshire Yeomanry to form the 8th Yeomanry Brigade of the 4th Division of Auxiliary Cavalry, rather than scattered independent troops. The Lichfield and Walsall troops formed "A" squadron, the Newcastle and Stafford Troops formed "B" squadron, Anglesey (Burton) and Uttoxeter Troops formed "C" and Himley and Wolverhampton Troops formed "D".

The first of the County's Yeoman to fight overseas were in the 6th and 106th companies of the 4th Battalion Imperial Yeomanry. The first contingent of the Regiment, consisting of 64 Yeoman and 50 specially enlisted civilians and volunteers, sailed for South Africa late in 1899, fighting their first action at Thabanchu in April 1900. Their most notable engagement was at Senekal from the 26th to 28th June. Three of the contingent died of wounds, eleven others of disease, and fifty others were invalided home. Major Bromley-Davenport (descendant of the previously mentioned Colonel) and Captain T.A. Wright-Boycott, received D.S.Os. When the war ended, the Staffordshire Yeomanry embarked for England, arriving home on 11th August 1902.

A Field Officer's tunic c. 1893-1914.

In October 1915 the Regiment again sailed to fight overseas, this time to Egypt where it joined the North Midland Mounted Brigade as part of the Western Frontier

Staffordshire Yeomanry cap badge, with Queen's Crown, as adopted for wear by the Regiment's ordinary ranks. This particular badge was worn officially until the end of the Second World War.

A Staffordshire Yeomanry soldier wearing Queen's crown cap badge, aboard a Lee/Grant tank just prior to the Battle of El-Alamein in World War II.

Force. At the end of March 1917, after three arduous months in the Sinai Peninsular, the Regiment advanced into Palestine, playing a notable part in the first battle of Gaza, and the second battle of Gaza which, though failing, prevented enemy reinforcements from the east.

In October the Regiment, as part of the newly formed Yeomanry Division, took part in the capture of Beersheba, leading to the fall of Gaza on November 7th. The next nine months were spent harassing the enemy in the hills North East of Jerusalem.

In September 1918, the Regiment played a prominent role in the capture of Damascus and the final collapse of the Turkish Army.

A 1917 casualty death plaque trio of Emil Leonard Dow Atkin, one of 73 Staffordshire Yeomanry World War I other ranks casualties.

Three
The History of the 38th Foot (1st Staffordshire Regiment) from 1705 to 1881 when it became the 1st Battalion of the South Staffordshire Regiment

A regiment of foot was formed by Colonel Luke Lillingston at the Kings Head public house in Bird Street, Lichfield in 1705. Two years later this regiment embarked for the West Indies where it remained for 58 years! The reason for this is not very clear. The unfortunate regiment may have been forgotten by the higher home command, or punished for the part some of its soldiers took in a rebellion in Antigua, but the

COLONEL LUKE LILLINGSTON RAISED A REGIMENT OF FOOT AT THE KING'S HEAD ON THE 25th MARCH 1705. THIS REGIMENT BECAME THE 38th FOOT IN 1751.. AND WAS GIVEN THE TITLE OF THE 1st STAFFORDSHIRE REGIMENT IN 1782. IN 1881 THE 38th FOOT BECAME THE 1st BN. THE SOUTH STAFFORDSHIRE REGIMENT.

probable reason was the need to keep soldiers in the West Indies which was then a valuable possession, and the main scene of fighting between the French, and later the Spanish, and Britain. Fighting was not the only task; these versatile soldiers also manned His Majesty's ships, helped in building and manning smaller ships and in fighting against the vigorously suppressed piracy that infested the seas in the area. Virtually all of this time the Regiment was split into detachments garrisoning the various islands.

Cheap and plentiful rum, the tropical climate, unsuitable clothing, yellow fever and other diseases took a heavy toll of the soldiers rather than enemy action. Despite much fighting with the French, Spaniards and pirates, GUADELOUPE and MARTINIQUE were the only battle honours awarded to the Regiment. The 'Holland patches' (commemorating the ragged/patched uniforms after 58 years in the West Indies) was worn by the South Staffordshire Regiment under their

Lillingston's Regiment in Antigua in 1709
(Rob Chapman, Flintlock Publishing).

badges, as a battle honour, for this unique and arduous service, until their amalgamation with the North Staffordshire Regiment in 1959.

In 1751 the Regiment became the 38th Foot. After the necessary recruitment on the Regiment's return to Lichfield, they went to Ireland, but after only a short spell there embarked to take part in the American War of Independence. The 38th Foot played a prominent part in the British victory of Bunkers Hill, and were stationed in New York. After assisting in the capture of the capital, the Regiment spent most of its time in garrison duties, missing the later fighting. The 38th Foot was given the title of the 1st Staffordshire Regiment in 1782.

This short stay abroad of only ten years was followed by the Regiment being posted to Stafford. Several interesting events were recorded in 1787. Seventy of the recruits deserted, most of whom came from Stafford and Wolverhampton. Perhaps Wolverhampton Wanderers had a home match! One of the first ever recorded Army Schools was started for the Regiment's children, and the Regiment's officers complained about not having been paid for seven years.

Yet another stay in Ireland was the prelude for a proportion of the Regiment visiting the West Indies again, and helping recapture

The 38th Regiment of Foot in Guadeloupe in 1759
(Rob Chapman, Flintlock Publishing).

Guadeloupe and Martinique along with the 64th foot, Second Staffordshire Regiment (later the 1st Battalion North Staffordshire Regiment). The newly formed 80th foot, Staffordshire Volunteers, the ranks coming mostly from the County Militia (later to become the 2nd Battalion, the South Staffordshire Regiment) were fighting alongside the remainder of the 38th foot in Flanders. Despite the troops gallant conduct, they were not prepared for the shocking winter of 1794/95 and disaster resulted. The higher command grossly neglected these troops who were clad in rags, and without great coats, and who must have bitterly envied their colleagues in the West Indies. As can be imagined, casualties were extremely high, the vast majority caused by the weather.

The 38th foot reforming in Ireland, were ordered after a few years to join the expedition to recapture the Cape of Good Hope. Though missing the main battle, they were involved in some sensational marching and probably an equal amount of swearing!

At the time, the majority of South America belonged to Spain with whom we were at war. The General and Admiral at the Cape decided on an attack on the Spanish Colonies. This was exceedingly high handed, even for those days. The siege of the captors of Buenos Aires by the indignant citizens followed the initial success of this campaign, resulting in the 38th foot being despatched to relieve the besieged troops.

For this to be achieved, the port of Monte Video's capture was necessary. Attacking at night, the 38th foot greatly distinguished themselves, but with the loss of their commanding officer. The unusually high state of the Regiment's discipline was demonstrated in the perfect order maintained following the port's capture. Despite the fighting prowess of the 38th foot, the ill-conceived campaign was a failure due to the Higher Command's shortcomings, and the expedition was withdrawn, but not before the Regiment earned the well deserved battle honour of MONTE VIDEO - 1806.

Napoleon's dominance of Europe meant that the 38th foot were now urgently required there. Because the Regiment was extremely well recruited, a second 38th was formed in 1804, and both took part in the Peninsula War in Spain and Portugal. The 1/38th took a prominent role initially fighting at Rolica and Vimiera, finishing with the retreat and defence of Corunna (the "Dunkirk" of this war). Later the 1/38th took part in the Walcheren expedition in Flanders. This invasion was as badly managed as the earlier invasion in which the 38th took part, and after some hard fighting the force was evacuated, chiefly due to malaria, and returned to Ireland.

Meanwhile the 2/38th were in the Peninsula under Wellesley, later to become the great Duke of Wellington. Raw as they were, they soon distinguished themselves at the battle of Busaco by a brilliant charge. The short lived 2/38th's most noteworthy exploit was achieved during the assault on the town of Badajos. The 2/38th was in the 5th Division ordered to capture its sector of the defences using ladders, a type of holding attack. Attacks to the main breaches were bloodily repulsed more than once, and though the castle had been captured by other troops, they could not break out of it. The 5th Division's attack was a success, but a French counter attack drove back the leading British Troops. The 2/38th drawn up in a line inside the town, formed a column to let the fugitives pass through them, reformed the line, fired a volley and advanced through the town driving all before them at the tip of the bayonet. With the breaches and the castle now attacked in the rear, resistance evaporated and Badajos was taken. The losses of the 2/38th were small, but the results vital, a very fine example of steady willing discipline saving a situation with far fewer casualties than if the discipline had been poor.

Salamanca was the next great battle concerning both 38ths who took a valiant part, even if their casualties were light by modern standards. This was Napoleon's first serious defeat, opening up Spain and later France to the British.

Both 38ths were engaged in the siege and retreat from Bargos and suffered severe casualties. This was to be the last battle of the 2/38th; orders were received to send its fit men to the 1st Battalion and then to return

2/38th Regiment at the battle of Badajos 1812.
(Rob Chapman, Flintlock Publishing).

The Army of India Medal 1799-1826,
with Ava bar, of Assistant Surgeon J. Dempster
of the 38th Foot, one of only 119 awarded
to the Regiment - and 25 years
after the campaign ended!

home for recruiting through 1812, but actually they disbanded in 1814.

In the meantime the 1/38th took part in the hard fought battle of Vittoria and the siege and capture of San Sebastian, losing many soldiers during the latter. They were then amongst the first British troops to invade France, distinguishing themselves in the battle of Nive, again suffering severe losses. It is of interest that British troops were much preferred by the French civilians to their own, who lived off the country, and in whose ranks were many foreigners.

Ten battle honours were won by the 38th Regiment in the Peninsular War, but were not indicative of their service. Companies were frequently attached to brigades and divisions, and even if the whole Regiment took part in a battle, they may not receive an honour for it.

Arriving too late in Flanders to fight at Waterloo, the Regiment formed part of the Army of Occupation in Paris for a time, returning to England to be stationed in Hastings, Portsmouth and Gloucester. From the latter they received a testimonial to their good behaviour. It is interesting to note flogging was unheard of in the Regiment, in contrast to one of the County's other regiments who rejoiced in the nickname of the "steel-backs".

Following a short stay in Ireland, on 18th June 1818 the Regiment embarked for the Cape of Good Hope, where they helped to quell a small Kaffir rising and successfully defeated overwhelming numbers of natives.

A move to India followed four years later, where they were garrisoned in Calcutta, then the capital. Trouble developed between the independent kingdom of Burma and the British Government in India, and, with considerable optimism, the King of Ava attempted to annex Bengal in India.

The 38th Regiment formed part of the Burma

The 38th Regiment in the Crimea in 1854
(Rob Chapman, Flintlock Publishing).

expedition, and spent four years fighting in this most unhealthy and unpleasant climate. One occasion saw the Regiment, together with the Somersets, defeat the main Burmese Army, earning the battle honour AVA. As usual most of the casualties were caused by disease like scurvy, the dreaded cholera and sunstroke.

The Regiment remained in Bengal for ten years. On their return, very few of the 38th who had embarked in 1818 disembarked in England in 1836. 1840 saw the Regiment embark for the Ionian Islands in the eastern Mediterranean. The next eight years saw service in Gibraltar, Jamaica and Halifax, Nova Scotia. In Jamaica, in 1848, they saw the only active service of this tour, with three hundred of the 38th foot taking part in a punitive expedition to Nicaragua. At Halifax misfortune befell the Regiment, their Barracks being totally destroyed by fire, The unhappy regiment lost everything and returned home in 1851.

1854 saw the Regiment embark for the Crimean War to prevent the Russians over-running Turkey, and obtaining the entrance to the Black Sea. For the first time in hundreds of years the British and French were on the same side, along with the Turks and Sardinians, (who were not very efficient or keen for a fight). The British Commander-in-Chief, an old Peninsular War veteran, had a habit of referring to the enemy as "the French" and it must have been a frequent embarrassment to all concerned.

38th hat numerals.

This war is chiefly remembered for the acute discomforts of the troops, who were not equipped for a winter campaign and the resultant appalling hardships, and also for the Women's Nursing Services under Florence Nightingale.

Despite the discomfort, the 38th foot took a very full part in the war, fighting at the battles of Alma, Inkerman and the siege and capture of Sevastopol, for all of which they received Battle Honours. The Regiment's experienced and humane Commanding Officer ensured those in his command suffered far less than most from disease, despite which they must have been well pleased to return to England in 1856.

Queen Victoria's inspection at Aldershot preceded the Regiment going again to Ireland. However this tour of duty was short lived, the Mutiny in India having flared up.

A contemporary three band Enfield Musket and bayonet, as would have been used by the Regiment.

The Regiment landed in Calcutta in November 1857, moving by forced marches to Cawnpore just in time to take part in a battle in which a party of rebels from Gwalior were decisively defeated.

After the escort of married families besieged in Agra, the Regiment was commanded by Sir Colin Campbell during the recapture of Lucknow. With surprisingly few casualties they helped storm the fortifications held by the mutineers and later received the battle honour LUCKNOW.

An India Mutiny Medal to drummer S. Irwin of the 38th foot with the "LUCKNOW" bar.

A Long Service and Good Conduct medal awarded to 513 Pte. T. Mardell on the 1st December 1876.

A Crimea, Turkish Crimean and Turkish Order of Medijidie awarded to Captain S G Quicke 38th foot, who was present at Inkerman, Sebastopol, and commanded the Volunteer sharpshooters, attacking and occupying the cemetery at Sevastopol on the 18th June.

Spending a further 15 years in India, the Crimea and Mutiny veterans must have wondered when they would see their homes again.

In early 1872 the Regiment returned, having spent the previous six years serving in four different stations, and were not surprised to hear in 1877 that it was again to move to Ireland.

To the Regiment's old "sweats", Ireland must have been more familiar than home. After three more years the Regiment then moved to Malta. Here their title was changed from the 38th foot (First Staffordshire Regiment) to become the 1st Battalion, The South Staffordshire Regiment, while the 80th (Staffordshire Volunteers) became the 2nd Battalion the South Staffordshire Regiment.

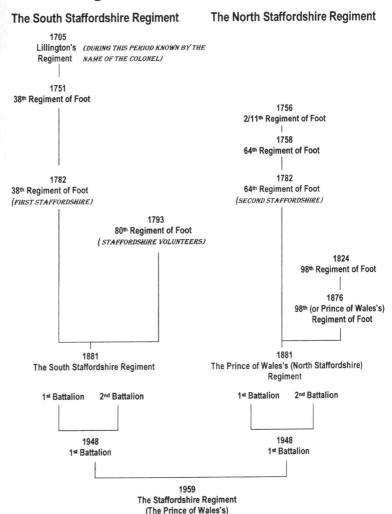

The Regular Staffordshire Regiments

The South Staffordshire Regiment   **The North Staffordshire Regiment**

1705
Lillington's *(DURING THIS PERIOD KNOWN BY THE*
Regiment *NAME OF THE COLONEL)*

1751
38th Regiment of Foot

1756
2/11th Regiment of Foot

1758
64th Regiment of Foot

1782
38th Regiment of Foot
(FIRST STAFFORDSHIRE)

1782
64th Regiment of Foot
(SECOND STAFFORDSHIRE)

1793
80th Regiment of Foot
(STAFFORDSHIRE VOLUNTEERS)

1824
98th Regiment of Foot

1876
98th (or Prince of Wales's)
Regiment of Foot

1881
The South Staffordshire Regiment

1881
The Prince of Wales's (North Staffordshire)
Regiment

1st Battalion   2nd Battalion

1st Battalion   2nd Battalion

1948
1st Battalion

1948
1st Battalion

1959
The Staffordshire Regiment
(The Prince of Wales's)

Contemporary excavated ordinary ranks shako plates of the 38th Foot.

A rank and file Glengarry badge 1874-1881 of the 64th Foot.

An officer's blue cloth, home service helmet plate of the 64th Foot c1878-1881.

Four
The History of the 64th Foot (2nd Staffordshire Regiment) from 1758 to 1881 when it became the 1st Battalion of the North Staffordshire Regiment

At the outbreak of the Seven Years War in 1756 it was decided to expand various regiments into double battalion regiments. Amongst those selected was the 11th Foot, later to become the Devonshire Regiment. This did not find favour for long, the 2nd battalions becoming independent by a decision put into effect by a War Office Order dated 21st April 1758. On that day the 2nd battalion the 11th Regiment became the 64th Foot.

Colonel the Honourable John Barrington from the 2nd Foot Guards was appointed Colonel, and Wollaston Pym the Lieutenant Colonel. It was probably Barrington who requested that the Regiment should adopt black facings - one of very few line Regiments to use the colour.

The 64th was almost immediately ordered to embark for an expedition to the West Indies. Coincidentally, both the 38th Foot and the 64th Foot were awarded the same first battle honour. Lying fifty miles south of Antigua was the French held island of Guadeloupe. This was the target for this expeditionary force. Colonel Barrington was largely responsible for the campaign's successful conclusion with the capture of Guadeloupe (after the General had died), and after much hard fighting. For their services during this difficult and unhealthy campaign the 64th received - after a short delay of only 150 years! - the battle honour: GUADELOUPE 1759.

The 64th sailed to England soon after the capture of Guadeloupe, leaving behind its fit soldiers, and required 787 rank and file to complete its numbers, though officers, sergeants and drummers were nearly up to strength. A year in Suffolk then saw the 64th move to Northern Scotland, the number of dead, sick and discharged showing it was still suffering from the after effects of sickness in the West Indies. A move to Ireland followed three years in Scotland where the Regiment remained until sent to America.

Boston was an unpleasant station for the 64th, being the centre of American discontent. It was probably a great relief to be transferred to Halifax, Nova Scotia, two years later. The 64th were back to Boston in 1772, but this time stationed at Castle William, on an island off the harbour. 1775 saw things come to a head in America and hostilities with the colonists break out; but the 64th remained at Castle William. In March General Howe, now commanding the British troops, decided to abandon Boston, withdrawing to Halifax to establish a base for operations against New York. The 64th was the last to embark, mining Castle William's fortifications, and thus the last British troops to set foot in the state of Massachusetts.

The 64th took part in operations to capture New York and then accompanied the British army to Philadelphia, taking a part in the decisive victory of Brandywine. Later, the 64th took part in raids from New York, going down to South Carolina; it was present at the siege of Charleston and distinguished itself in the hard fought battle of Eutaw Springs.

In 1782, to encourage recruitment which had fallen off owing to this unpopular war, it was decided to give regiments of the line a territorial designation. The 64th became the 2nd Staffordshire, the 38th, the 1st Staffordshire. Both were more or less based at Lichfield and continued there ever after.

Following the end of the war in America, the 64th went to Jamaica, returning to England in 1784 for some very necessary recruitment. With the outbreak of war with France the 64th embarked for the West Indies in 1793 . Again the flank companies (light and grenadier companies) were detached to serve in separate units. Guadeloupe and Martinique had both been handed back to the French, so the unfortunate British units could presumably have an opportunity to capture them again! Guadeloupe fell reasonably easily, Martinique being far harder to capture. The British including the 64th and composite battalions of the light and grenadier companies of all the Regiments present suffered six weeks of hard fighting before Fort Bourbon - the principal stronghold, fell to a vigorous assault. The 64th took a prominent role in this well run campaign, where the combined operations for once worked brilliantly, thanks to the efficiency and lack of jealousy of the naval and military commanders.

The 64th at Eutaw Springs in 1781
(Rob Chapman, Flintlock Publishing).

This campaign was unfortunately marred by the inevitable appalling loss of life from disease, and further hindered by slave risings on both British and French Islands as a result of the French Revolution, but the 64th deservedly won its second battle honour: MARTINIQUE 1794.

Following Martinique's capture the 64th had more fighting in the West Indies. The rebellion of 1798 in Ireland meant they did not have much peace in Britain either. 1800 saw the 64th return to the West Indies, helping capture various Danish and French Islands and then also having a go at the Dutch. Britain was not short of enemies to fight at the time! In the capture of St. Martin, north of St. Kitts Nevis, the 64th's conduct was highly praised. Occupation of the Danish Virgin Isle of St. Cruz moved the inhabitants to present them with silver trophies, that are still in the 64th's successor's possession.

Moving south the 64th took a leading role in capturing St. Lucia, leading the assault on the principal fortress of Morne Fortunee and earning the battle honour: ST. LUCIA 1803 in the process. Moving ever southwards Tobago was captured. An attack made on the Guianas on mainland South America, resulted in the capture of the valuable territory of British Guiana. The assault on Surinam (Dutch Guiana) was also successful, but it was later handed back. At New Amsterdam, the 64th captured an important fort, crossed the river and annexed another two forts which remained part of British Guiana. The capture of the fort led to the surrender of the town and eventually all of Surinam. Garrisoned by the 64th for the next nine years, silver tokens were presented by the 64th's former enemies as a gesture of respect and admiration for the friendly well behaved officers and men, and these are still in the Regiment's successor's possession, as is the battle honour, SURINAM, trophies of a hard, long and almost forgotten campaign.

The 64th arrived in Belgium too late to fight at Waterloo, and instead formed part of the British Army of Occupation in France. The good conduct of the 64th and the British army as a whole, was in stark contrast to that of their other allies.

The now 2nd Staffordshire Regiment left France in 1816, stayed two years in Plymouth, then moved to Gibraltar. The CO's daughter presented new colours, which was an unusual break with normal traditions of the presentation by royalty or a distinguished military officer.

An officer's coatee button of the 2nd Staffordshire Regiment 64th Foot.

In Gibraltar all ranks suffered with lung and eye troubles caused by loose sand and strong winds during the building of new barracks and batteries. The 64th were kept hard at work for the next nine years in this then, very unhealthy and confined station. Surely this was far too long.

1827 saw the 64th embark for Ireland, to Galway, Dublin and then Belfast, finding numerous detachments. During this period and for many years to come the 64th recruited largely from Ireland, as indeed did many other infantry regiments.

Whether it was because the 64th liked the West Indies, or that Horse Guards and later the War Office was impressed by the Regiment's excellent behaviour is uncertain, but 1834 saw the 64th again embark for Jamaica, its fifth visit to the West Indies. The slaves had by then been freed and this resulted in an exciting time with some disorder, but it was quelled by the firm but tactful 64th. Despite frequent station changes, yellow fever still caused many deaths. Embarkation to Halifax, Nova Scotia from this beautiful but deadly island was to everbody's relief. The 64th had to find detachments because of lack of accommodation rather than internal security, partly because the wooden barracks frequently burned down. The town was plagued with numerous fires and the good conduct of the 64th along with their valuable assistance in putting them out earned the 64th warm praise.

1843 saw the 64th leave Halifax for England, one of the 64th's ships striking a reef on their first day. The soldiers being below, their instinct was to get on deck, but it was explained that this might founder the ship, so all ranks remained quietly below amongst the rising water. The vessel was beached and all were saved, in due course receiving warm praise for their discipline and courage from the Great Duke of Wellington himself.

From Portsmouth the 64th arrived at Weedon after a remarkable railway journey, for those times, of just one day. At Northampton the 64th demonstrated their skill born from practice, by extinguishing a dangerous fire. Birmingham, Coventry, Wolverhampton, Hanley, Burslem and Newcastle-under-Lyme had detachments on recruiting as well as police duties.

An inevitable move to Ireland followed, for four years, with lots of internal moves and detachments. Four years later the 64th were ready for embarkation to India.

Stationed at Poona much suffering was caused in the 64th by dysentery and cholera, and its move to Karachi in 1849 saw cholera break out again. The 64th was therefore sent in two wings to cholera camps. Monotony and discomfort encouraged the disease. The move to Hyderabad, in Sind multiplied the 64th's problems with the mud barracks washing away in the monsoon, and the Regiment forced to live in dripping tents. A proposed expedition against a rebellious Rajah concentrated the whole Regiment at Hyderabad, but came to nothing causing disappointment in all ranks. The 64th then moved to Karachi en route to Begaum in 1853, and was inspected six times by the District Commander in its eighteen months there.

Part of a trunk lock, named to Captain Hinchcliff, 64th Regiment, who was promoted Captain on 8th Feb. 1856.

At the conclusion of the Crimean War a smaller campaign was conducted in Persia to which the 64th were sent from India in 1856. December saw the 64th landing near Bushire on the Persian Gulf, and they immediately attacked the Persians, at Reshire village, capturing it with a dashing bayonet charge. They marched to Bushire and then made defensive positions after its surrender following the naval bombardment.

Some 46 miles away, a column including the 64th, attacked a strong enemy post. The distance was covered in forty hours despite the troops being heavily laden and moving over difficult country in cold, driving rain. The Persians retreated before the intended attack. However the column still took or destroyed an enormous quantity of the enemy's munitions and stores. The lack of these seriously inhibited the enemy's ability to wage war. A strong force of the enemy were decidedly beaten when the returning column was attacked at the battle of Koosh-ab, chiefly by the British guns and cavalry, though three companies had a brief engagement suffering 20 casualties against 700 Persians left dead. The rugged country inland hampered movement of the British troops forcing them to sail up the Shatt-al Arab estuary leading to the easy capture of the important town of Mohammerek, and again the capture of large quantities of munitions and stores.

Reforming at Ahwaz the enemy was pursued to the river port by the flank companies of both the British Regiments involved. The large stature of the men of the 64th greatly dismayed the Persians, who again fled before they could be engaged leaving their food and munitions behind. That which was not required by the British column was destroyed. On returning the column learned that peace was to be signed, and this brief campaign was over. The 64th were awarded the rare battle honours: RESHIRE, BUSHIRE, KOOSH-AB and PERSIA for this brief but well managed campaign.

They arived in Bombay from Persia in May 1857 to find that a part of the Indian Army had rebelled. The Indian Mutiny had started and the 64th were at once ordered to Calcutta, presumably by steamer; and it took a fortnight to reach there. Detachments moved north-west by bullock train and steamers, where companies guarded disaffected towns. The main body joined a column at Allahabad under General Havelock, who had until now been handicapped by unreliable troops and lack of transport.

An India General Service Medal with the bar "Persia" to F. Doherty - 64th Foot.

The 64th found 54 men to assist the advanced artillery heading for Cawnpore. General Havelock received news of the fall of Cawnpore to the mutineers whilst on the march, and realising that his advance guard was in mortal danger, pushed on with the main column despite the terrible heat. In fact, the mutineers from Cawnpore were preparing to ambush the advance guard, not knowing the main column was hot on their heels.

Armed with superior rifles and artillery and looking for revenge for the massacre at Cawnpore, the British inflicted a crushing defeat on the mutineers, capturing many guns. Though seven men of the 64th died of sunstroke, because they were armed with their longer range rifles, there were no battle casualties for the Regiment. Later, however, during the advance on Cawnpore, many men were killed in fighting to take the strong rebel position guarding the town.

Despite determined and accurate gunfire, a gallant charge by the 64th finally captured the enemy

The 64th at Cawnpore in 1857
Rob Chapman, Flintlock Publishing

positions, opening the way to Cawnpore. By this time the 64th had marched 126 miles under a July sun and fought four actions in ten days.

With Agra and Lucknow besieged, and Dehli in rebel hands, there was still much to do. Havelock tried twice to advance on Lucknow, and, despite beating the mutineers in three actions in which the 64th took their full share, he was forced to retire to Cawnpore each time. The third advance left the 64th's headquarter's company behind garrisoning Cawnpore. The advance, with a strong detachment of the 64th, entered the residency at Lucknow, but could not fight their way out. The gallant party rendered much assistance during the following siege.

Reinforcements were en route, and in November a new force under Sir Colin Campbell relieved Lucknow, picking up a detachment of the 64th at Alambagh on their way.

In the meantime the 64th's headquarter's company garrisoning Cawnpore were attacked by the Gwalior mutineers and only just managed to hold out. The 64th's desperate counter-attack cost the lives of the C.O. and six other senior officers, but saved the day. The Gwalior mutineers were defeated on Sir Colin Campbell's return, and the 64th then took their share in clearing Northern India of rebels.

| An Indian Mutiny Medal with the bar "Defence of Lucknow" to Thos. McNamara 64th Foot - a member of Havelock's first column. | An Indian Mutiny Medal with the bar "Lucknow" to Thos. McNamara 64th Foot - a member of Campbell's second column. |

During the last action at Cawnpore, where the Regiment lost its senior officers in their attack on the enemy guns, Drummer Flynn won the V.C. For his outstanding courage, Lieut. O'Grady was strongly recommended for the honour but did not receive it.

If the award of battle honours for the Persian War had seemed over generous, this could not be said for the Mutiny honour. The reward for all their hard fighting and long hot marches was just the one battle honour: LUCKNOW.

Ten years, in Persia and India, had preceded two years for the 64th in Karachi. Now it was to return home and it opened its ranks to soldiers wishing to leave India. It attracted 332 NCOs and men, most taking the places of those of the 64th staying. The Regiment was still well below strength on its return to England in 1861, but soon filled its ranks, though it remained continually on the move.

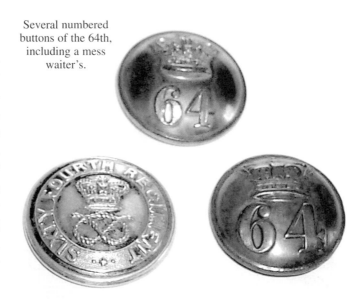

Several numbered buttons of the 64th, including a mess waiter's.

The next five years saw the 64th serve at Dover, Aldershot, Gosport, Portsmouth and Manchester - the last the usual station before Ireland. 1866 saw the 64th at Templemore, Tipperary, with the usual multitude of detachments. In 1867, the 64th were in Malta for five years, returning to Ireland in 1872, now commanded by Lieut. Colonel De Courcy Hamilton V.C.

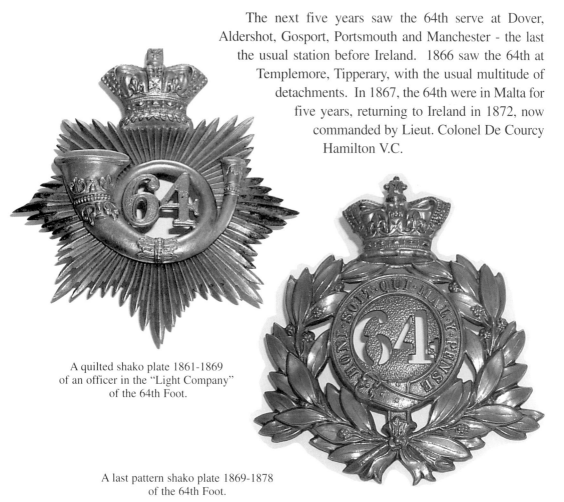

A quilted shako plate 1861-1869 of an officer in the "Light Company" of the 64th Foot.

A last pattern shako plate 1869-1878 of the 64th Foot.

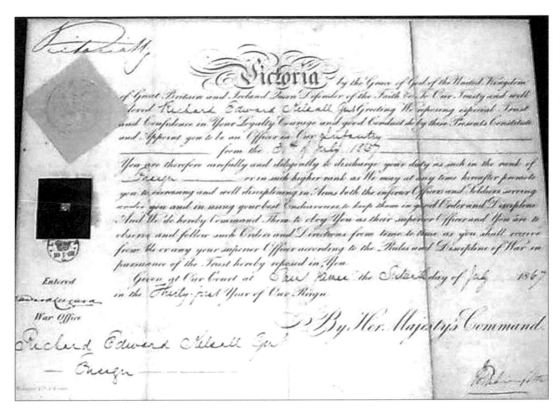

A officer's commission for ensign Richard Edward Kelsall, of the 64th Regiment, dated 31st July 1867.

The Depot of the 98th joined the 64th at Limerick under the linked battalion system; the combined Depots of the Staffordshire Regiments moving to Lichfield in 1880 on the construction of their barracks.

Though duties in Ireland were unpopular and unpleasant, a testimonial from the Mayor and council of Limerick bear witness to the 64th's excellent conduct.

In 1874 the 64th embarked for Glasgow, regaining possession of its very first colour (a very old custom had been for the retiring C.O to take it). Four quick moves to Portsmouth, Aldershot, Colchester and the Channel Isles followed the year in Scotland.

In 1881 the Infantry of the line reorganised into two battalion regiments with a territorial area and permanent depot within the recruitment area. The 64th and 98th became the 1st and 2nd Battalions The Prince of Wales's (North Staffordshire Regiment), changing to the North Staffordshire Regiment (The Prince of Wales's) after the 1914-1918 war. The change was not particularly popular and some regiments continued to use their old numerals for many years after, and there was often rivalry, not always friendly, between the two units of the same regiment.

Five
The History of the 80th Foot (Staffordshire Volunteers) from 1793 to 1881 when it became the 2nd Battalion of the South Staffordshire Regiment

Revolutionary France, after her execution of King Louis XVI and Queen Marie Antoinette in 1793, quickly declared war on Britain, Spain and the Nederlands. With such a serious threat to Britain, the Government decided a lot more troops were required to defend Britain and to fight the French on the European Mainland.

This culminated in the British government asking for the formation of new Regiments. Lord Henry William Paget jumped at the chance to form his own Regiment, and although he was only twenty-five years of age and had very little military experience, other than serving in his father's own militia, he did at least come from a military family. Following a meeting with Prime Minister William Pitt, Henry Paget resigned from his father's militia and took up a Lieutenant-Colonelcy in his new Regiment, the 80th foot, in 1793.

The 80th Regiment had been first raised in 1758 as the 80th (Light Armed) Regiment of Foot but was disbanded in 1764. It was raised again as the 80th (Royal Edinburgh Volunteers) in 1778 and disbanded twelve years later. The 1793 80th Foot was the third Regiment to be designated 80th, but the only one to have a connection with Staffordshire.

Lord Henry William Paget's father was the fabulously wealthy Lord Uxbridge, and he greatly financed the 80th Regiment. Lord Uxbridge not only allowed the transfer of many soldiers from the militia (hence Staffordshire Volunteers), from his vast estates in the centre of Staffordshire, but he also presented commissions (which he could have sold), and also paid for much of the uniform, equipment and weapons, from his ample resources.

The soldiers of the 80th would wear red tunics, blue trousers, and have yellow facings, collars and cuffs to distinguish them from other Regiments.

The 700 men of all ranks of the 80th Foot, which also included Paget's two uncles (who had also joined the Regiment with the ranks of Major), were ordered to Guernsey via Chatham because of the French threat to the Channel Islands in 1794. Wanting to see action, Paget was unhappy with this posting and with his family's connections obtained a posting to mainland Europe.

In this awful Flanders campaign of 1794/1795 (coincidentally along with the 38th Foot, 1st Staffordshire Regiment), the shocking neglect by the authorities at home, and the very hard winter reduced the British

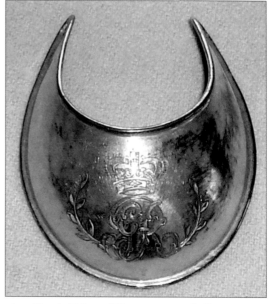

An officer's Universal Pattern gorget, similar to ones that officers of the 80th would have worn.

Army to a terrible state. Thousands of the ragged, half starved soldiers, and many of their wives and children, who in those days accompanied regiments on service, were frozen to death. Despite these incredible hardships and loss, the troops fought with great gallantry.

The Regiment returned to England with less than half its men fit for duty in 1795, and following a short recovery, embarked for the Isle of Dieu off the French coast. The 80th again lost many men and achieved very little.

With only the minimum of time to reform, the Regiment was now sent to the Cape of Good Hope in 1796. Here it had the most unusual task of capturing a Dutch naval squadron, and providing troops to serve on board these ships.

Revolutionary France, expanding its empire under Napoleon Bonaparte, now took control of Egypt. Seeing a threat to India, Britain decided to take on the French troops, sending the 80th foot, amongst other regiments, to India. They arrived in Trincomalee in Ceylon in 1801, joining the General, Sir Ralph Abercomby. The French soldiers were trapped, thanks to Nelson's decisive defeat of the French fleet at the Battle of the Nile, but this strong enemy force on the shorter route to India was not be ignored, and two British armies, one from the Mediterranean, and the other from India, were ordered to converge on Egypt. Included in the latter force was the 80th.

It was a tragic expedition because parts of the fleet were shipwrecked on the way there and back. The Army from India, had to march across the desert from the Red Sea to the Nile, and when they got there, they were too late to take part in the fighting. After a year in Egypt they marched back. The British and Indian governments treated the troops generously and the 80th, for its part in the war in Egypt, 1801, received the battle honour, The Sphinx, superscribed EGYPT.

Various 80th officer's coatee and other ranks numbered buttons

Returning to India, the Regiment saw much fighting in South India, but gained no battle honours, and more importantly, for the troops, no prize money. In 1816, the 80th were ordered back to Britain for Home Service, but all privates fit for duty remained in India. The first job, for the Regiment back in Britain, was to recruit, and this only took a few months to reach a full establishment of men again.

Normal policing duties followed in England and Scotland, and the 80th were stationed in Edinburgh when they were ordered to march to Liverpool to embark for Ireland. From 1821 the Regiment was in Gibraltar, Malta and the Ionian Islands for the next ten years, after which they embarked to return to Britain for policing duties in England and Ireland again.

In 1836, the 80th was ordered to escort convicts to Australia. Many criminals were either hanged or deported in those days - there were few prisons. The 80th Foot made the long and dreary journey as wardens, in small detachments. In Australia, road gangs and prisons had to be supervised, and in their seven years in New South Wales, including detachments to Norfolk Island and other parts of Australasia, the Regiment helped in the early history of the continent.

American and French ships were found to be cruising in the vicinity of the islands of New Zealand. At that time only North Island belonged to Britain and this was administered from New South Wales; South Island had not been annexed. A detachment of 83 rank and file, with four officers, under the command of Major Bunbury, was sent to the territory to hoist the Union Jack at various prominent sites. All of New Zealand now came into the British Empire.

Before they left the continent, any sentences inflicted by Court Martial were remitted by the Governor of the Australian Colonies, as a reward for the Regiment's good behaviour there. Being Colonel to the Regiment may have influenced his decision! Some of the first settlers with connections with Staffordshire were four rank and file soldiers who took their discharge whilst in New Zealand.

In 1844 the 80th embarked for Agra in India. One of the four ships *The Briton* carried Major Bunbury, three companies and their families. They took a short cut and ran into a hurricane and were wrecked on the Andaman Islands in the Bay of Bengal. The 800 ton ship was firmly wedged on a mangrove swamp before those on board realised what had happened, so strong was the gale. Those on board were further amazed to find another troopship also wrecked close by. Fifty days were spent in this inhospitable island, inhabited by cannibals, until they were rescued.

On their eventual arrival at Agra, one third of the Regiment was in hospital, until the prospect of active

An 80th officer's shoulder belt plate c. 1810.

service seemed to prove a better cure than the medical staff could make. In 1845 the 80th were on the Punjab borders, the then frontier of British India. The Sikh inhabitants were a war-like group, and angry at the British occupation of nearby provinces. The small number of the British troops encouraged the Sikhs, whose formidable artillery both outnumbered and outranged the British guns, to invade British India. Opposing the Sikh army were a mere 7,000 British troops together with a few thousand unreliable native infantry. When combined they were far less in number than any one of the three Sikh armies preparing to attack them.

The first engagement was at Moodkee. The Sikhs were driven back with heavy loss, but a tenth of the British were killed - a serious blow to an already small force. The Sikhs withdrew to their stronghold of Ferozeshah while the exhausted British lay on the cold ground

they had taken, under constant artillery fire. The Governor General of India, who was present with the British army, called upon the 80th to silence one heavy gun that was a particular nuisance. The weary troops assembled and moved into the darkness. There was a rousing cheer as they charged, put the gun out of action and returned leaving their dead, but not their wounded, behind them in the darkness.

The next day the Sikhs were decisively beaten, losing most of their guns. The 80th again suffered severe losses. For their gallantry the 80th were highly praised by the Governor General, the Commander-in-Chief, and later by the Duke of Wellington in the House of Lords.

An other ranks helmet plate of the 80th.

A dashing right flank attack by the 80th proved decisive in the final defeat of the Sikhs at Sobraon. The Sikhs' loss was so great, it was deliberately recorded after the war. The 80th was awarded the Battle Honours: MOODKEE, FEROZESHAH and SOBRAON.

The Battle of Ferozeshah is still annually commemorated by the Staffordshire Regiment when the colours are handed over to the sergeants in memory of the capture of the Sikh standard, in this battle, by Colour-Sergeant Kirkland. This together with the two taken at Sobraon are still in the Regimental Chapel in Lichfield Cathedral.

Six years later the 80th embarked from India for Burma, for the Second Burmese War,

An other ranks shoulder belt plate

LEFT: Sutlej Campaign Medal of William Reeves who died of wounds 04/02/1846, so there is no Sobraon bar.

RIGHT: Sutlej Campaign medal of John Ross who received the Ferozeshuhur and Sobraon bar.

LEFT: India General Service Campaign medal of Sergeant D. King with the Pegu bar.

RIGHT: The India Mutiny Campaign medal of Wals Clements who was not entitled to any bars to his medal because the Regiment was only entitled to the Central India bar. This medal probably has an 'added' UN-entitled bar (buyer beware!)

the Burmese King having broken the earlier treaty of 1826. This short war saw the successful storming of Rangoon, Pegu and Prome, and for their part, the 80th were awarded the battle honour, PEGU.

The Regiment returned to Britain to recruit in 1854. They were in the Cape Colony in 1856, and then went to India on the outbreak of the Mutiny. Arriving in Calcutta, in February 1858, they went as fast as the slow travel conditions would allow, to Allahabad. A detachment of the 80th was sent as a flying column chasing a party of rebels, before the 80th was completely assembled, but the mutineers escaped across a wide river.

On another occasion, a hard pressed British column was rescued by two companies of the 80th who had been acting as Camel Corp. In a dramatic and last minute action, the 80th held a river. against the enemy, and then, thanks to their camels, were able to overtake and annihilate them.

At the close of the Mutiny, the 80th were involved in 'mopping up' patrols and expeditions, in various detachments, with endless marches in the intense heat, very often on wildgoose chases. But at the end, once engaged, very few of the rebels escaped. The 80th received the battle honour, CENTRAL INDIA for its long year of difficult warfare in this little known final phase of the India Mutiny War.

After several years in India the 80th returned home to undergo a tour of Ireland. In 1866 the Regiment embarked again for India, joining the Bhutan Field Force to subdue the troublesome Bhutanese and prevent their raids into British Territories. Following this short punitive war, the 80th re-embarked for home to undergo further tours of England and Ireland, mainly irksome police duties.

In 1872 the 80th Regiment was in Singapore, with three companies moving on to Hong Kong in less than a year to avenge the murder of a British resident by the Ismail of Malaya, in

The India General Service Campaign medal of 396 T Chatfield with the Bhootan bar.

The Perak and South Africa (Zulu War) Campaign Medal pair of 108 Pte M. Arthurs (This Perak bar of the India General Service Campaign Medal, was one of only 300 to the 80th Regiment)

1

the British Territory of Perak. In the short campaign that followed, two enemy guns were captured which are still in the modern Staffordshire Regiment's possession.

In 1876 the 80th were ordered to embark for South Africa, finally arriving in Natal after a typically eventful journey, with the outbreak of measles and resultant quarantine. A warlike tribe, the Zulus, threatened to invade Natal. In the Sekukuni campaigns of 1878 and 1879, the Regiment guarded the frontiers of Zululand, and the major part of the 80th formed one of five columns sent into this turbulent area, in the north of the country, to engage and defeat the Zulus in battle.

At Isandhlwana, part of one of these columns, consisting of approximately 858 officers, NCOs and men, predominantly but not exclusively of the 24th South Warwickshire Regiment, and 500 blacks, was annihilated with very few survivors. This regiment did not become the South Wales Borderers until after the 1881 re-organisation. There is also a mistaken belief, fuelled by a certain film, that they received the most VCs, 11, in one day, at Rorkes Drift. This was beaten by 15 VCs at the Battle of Inkerman during the Crimean War, on 5th November 1854.

With the 24th at the Battle of Isandhlawana there was a detachment of mounted infantry from the 80th Regiment, including Acting Quarter-Master Sergent (H.Q.Staff) Henry Thompson and Sergeant William Johnson, who were killed in action, and seven privates, five of whom were killed. Among the survivors was Private S. Wassall, who seeing Private T. Westwood, also of the 80th, drowning in the swollen river, re-entered the water, got to the Zulu side under close and heavy rifle fire, and showers of assegai spears, and rescued him. Thus the initial Victoria Cross won on this disastrous day did not go to the 24th, but to the 80th for the heroism of Private S. Wassall. This was the first VC to be won by the Regiment.

The 80th 'Mounted Infantry' at the Battle of Isandhlwana (Rob Chapman, Flintlock Publishing).

A second Victoria Cross was to follow shortly, when a company of the 80th on escort duty, were attacked at night at the Ntombi River, on 12th March 1879, by a horde of Zulus. The company were in the main massacred. The few survivors were rallied by Colour Sergeant Booth, who covered the survivors' retreat across the river and conducted a fighting withdrawal back to camp.

Full and exacting revenge was obtained by the 80th Regiment. The chief who had led the attack at the Ntombi River was killed by an officer of the 80th, and the Regiment held the position of honour in the front square which destroyed the Zulu army at the battle of Ulundi.

Major Tucker, later Lieutenant-General Sir Charles, and Colonel of the South Staffordshire Regiment for many years, allowed the fanatical Zulus to get within close range before firing the devastating volleys that the British Army was renowned for. Flesh and blood could not stand such fire. A single Martini Henry rifle bullet accounted for three and four Zulus at a time. The brave Zulus now retreated, only to be fiercely attacked by the British Cavalry and completely routed.

Martini Henry bullet similar to those issued to the 80th during this campaign

The end of the Zulu Wars did not see the end of the work of the 80th in South Africa. A detachment helped subdue another native chief who had defied Briton and Boer alike for several years. By this firm action on the way to embark, it was considered that Major Tucker and the 80th delayed the 1st Boer War that would eventually break out in 1881. For its gallant services in South Africa, the Regiment received its final Battle Honour: SOUTH AFRICA 1878-1879.

The Regiment was the last Staffordshire County regiment to see action before the 1881 Line Regiment Reorganisation of two battalion regiments. When eventually they reached Dublin the 80th were in rags, many of the troops not having shaved in three years, but it did not prevent Major Tucker marching them through the City, the inhabitants giving an enthusiastic reception regardless of their state.

In 1881 the Infantry were re-organised into two battalion regiments with territorial titles and permanent depots within the recruitment area. The 38th and 80th became the 1st and 2nd Battalions, The South Staffordshire Regiment.

In the fullness of time the title of Lord Uxbridge had been inherited by Lord Henry William Paget, on the death of his father. He was destined to become an experienced military campaigner and distinguished cavalry officer, even having a hand in the development of the 'Paget', later to become the New Land Pattern, cavalry (flintlock) pistol. He was second in command to Wellington, with the rank of Field Marshall, at the Battle of Waterloo, where he lost his right leg as a result of a cannon ball strike. Later he was created Marquis of Anglesey KG GCB. He could be very proud of his 80th Regiment of Foot's (Staffordshire Volunteers) achievements.

An other ranks Glengarry badge of the 80th.

Six
The History of the 98th Foot from 1824 to 1881 when it became the 2nd Battalion of the North Staffordshire Regiment

Following the battle of Waterloo, both the strength and training of the army fell to a low ebb, although its commitments in guarding the vast, and still growing, British Empire were steadily increasing. In 1824 it became apparent that the army had been cut too far and an Act of Parliament authorised the raising of some additional regiments, amongst which was the 98th Foot, formed in Chichester by Lieutenant-Colonel Mildmay Fane, formerly of the 61st Foot, who was to have a distinguished career in India and who became a general.

The first 98th Foot had also been raised in Chichester in 1760, and had fought at Martinique, Havana, and at the capture of Belle Isle in the Seven Years War, only to be disbanded in 1763. The second 98th was raised in 1779, serving as marines with the British fleet in the Bay of Bengal and with distinction in the Carnatic in India against Hyder Ali of Mysore, again, only to be disbanded in 1784. The third 98th Foot was the Argyllshire Highlanders raised in 1793, renumbered as the 91st Foot in 1798, and who were to become the 1st Argyll and Sutherland Highlanders in time. The next 98th Foot was raised in 1805, and served mainly in North America and was renumbered as the 97th Foot in 1815, only to be disbanded in 1818. Finally, there was the 98th Prince of Wales's Tipperary Regiment which was raised in 1805 as the 99th Foot and was renumbered in 1815. This regiment saw service, in Canada until it too was disbanded in 1818.

In April 1824 our latest 98th only numbered 90 strong, but was up to establishment by the 10th July. No particular recruiting area seems to have been allocated to this latest 98th Foot. Officers and NCOs were drafted from other units, but the men were young recruits from all over the kingdom. The first intake was probably English, but it is assumed that the later rank and file were Irish, most of whom were inexperienced and not used to military life. However it is to the Regiment's credit that, on leaving Chichester in December 1825 for the Cape Colony, the local magistrates congratulated the 98th Foot on their discipline in not requiring a single action by the civil authorities.

The 98th was to spend 13 years in the Cape Colony guarding the white settlers from the Kaffirs, and looking after convict gangs. No active service came their way. In 1829 Sir Harry Smith, who was to become the Commander-in Chief in South Africa, recorded that the 98th Foot was *"extremely well organised considering what a short time it had been raised"*. At the end of this tour, an officer on the half-pay list, Lieut. Colonel Colin Campbell, was appointed to command and was in command when the 98th Foot arrived home in good order in 1837. Although Campbell had served with distinction in the Peninsular War and had 25 years service, his Lieutenant Colonelcy still cost him the normal price of £1,300. However, Colin Campbell was later to win fame as the Commander-in Chief in India during the India Mutiny and he later became Field Marshal Lord Clyde.

The maintenance of civil order at home was for many years the main duty of the army, as these were troubled times in England with the Chartist disturbances gathering momentum. With the exception of the Bow Street Runners in London, there was virtually no police in

Britain (the parish constable was the nearest thing). Civil disturbances and riots had to be suppressed by either troops or the Yeomanry. This explains the many moves of regiments and, to some extent, the civilian population's dislike of the army, that would continue until a truly national force was established in the 1914-1918 World War.

Men very often enlisted for life in the Army, often losing touch with their kin, and it was often regarded as a disgrace when any decent man joined up, but the blandishments of the recruiting sergeant and the natural love of adventure, fortunately, often overcame family disapproval. Campbell was a great admirer of Sir John Moore, training the 98th Foot with his ideas in mind. The lack of complaints against his troops, on their marches between places such as Weedon, Manchester and Hull, delighted Campbell, despite there being plentiful supplies of liquor available to the 98th Foot.

The 98th Foot had a stay of two years at Newcastle-on-Tyne where there was a danger of Chartist riots, and were constantly called out to keep the peace. The regiment also had a detachment in the Isle of Man during most of this time. In 1841 the 98th Foot embarked for Ireland, but before the regiment had time to settle it was ordered to China. The First China War, sometimes known as the 'Opium War' had started; the British object was to open the Chinese ports to foreign trade, and reinforcements were needed.

The Recruiting Sergeant

The regiment embarked for China in the *Belleisle* from Plymouth on the 13th December 1842, a troopship designed to carry 850 people but actually with 1,277 on board, of whom 110 were women and children (six women per company were allowed to embark). It was very rough weather in the earlier part of the voyage, and the voyage lasted 164 days at sea in cramped conditions. It must have been an unfit unit which arrived in Hong Kong six months later, where the women and children disembarked.

The 98th remained on board and sailed up the Yangtse River, joining an expedition at Woosung to capture the old capital of Nanking, 160 miles further upstream. Lord Saltoun's

1842 Pattern British percussion cap
musket, similar to ones that the soldiers
of the 98th would have used.

1st Brigade, composed of the 26th and 98th Foot, the Bengal Volunteer Battalion and the 41st Madras Native Infantry, formed the flank companies.

Thirty miles below Nanking was the city of Chin-kiang-foo. This was to be the initial objective, but on their arrival, it was found that part of the Chinese force occupied two entrenched camps some distance away on a ridge. The 1st Brigade, including the 98th Foot, were ordered to attack these camps, the two other brigades attacking the city itself.

With the Light Company of the 98th as an advance guard, Saltoun's Brigade found themselves marching through paddy fields for about three and a half hours, dressed in their thick home service uniforms in the intense heat. Breasting a rise, divided by a small valley from the enemy's position, the advance guard discovered the Chinese had formed up in one body and struck their tents. Ineffective fire was opened and there was much blowing of bugles and shouting.

The 98th and Madras troops were sent by Saltoun to turn the Chinese left flank, the Bengal Volunteers to turn their right flank, whilst guns from a mountain battery opened fire on their centre. The Chinese wavered and fled. The 98th's Light Company pursued the Chinese but caught up with very few. In the engagement the 98th only had one man wounded, but the effects of the sun caused the men to drop like flies, and by nightfall thirteen of them were dead.

The remainder of the force had successfully stormed the city in the meantime. That night the first cholera cases occurred in the 98th Foot, and a week later, when the fit men of the 98th re-embarked for Nanking on a river steamer, upwards of 200 men, unfit for duty, were left behind on the Belleisle, which by this time was a floating hospital. The deaths had already reached 53.

On the 98th's arrival at Nanking, just as the attack was about to begin, overtures for peace stopped the fighting, but the negotiations dragged on for months. The Regiment was billeted in a temple alongside a creek, with swarms of malaria-carrying mosquitoes. There were many more deaths, and a very sick 98th was re-embarked on the Belleisle on the 3rd September.

The Regiment's first experience of active service had been an unfortunate one, with little opportunity to engage the enemy or win distinction. However the 98th Foot's efforts were rewarded with the battle honour, The DRAGON superscribed CHINA.

On the 29th September, the 98th Foot arrived in Hong Kong as a garrison, but with there being no accommodation on shore, they had to stay on board the Belleisle for the next four months. Colin Campbell reported at the end of December that his regiment had suffered the grim total of 283 deaths during the past six months and had 260 sick, most of whom would not recover.

Even on the Regiment's arrival in

The 98th in China in 1842 in heavy home service uniform. (Rob Chapman, Flintlock Publishing).

Stanley, the following February, things did not improve greatly. The following year, 1843, the garrison's death rate was some 25%; a shocking reminder of the suffering of British soldiers during peacetime "propping up the empire". The once fine regiment had now lost over 60% of its number, with many more sick, and the depot companies were brought out from home to augment its numbers.

At last, in 1845, Colin Campbell persuaded Headquarters to move the sorely stricken 98th to the comparatively healthy island of Chusan, south of Shanghai, where he had for some time been in command of the British garrison. The more temperate climate here soon enabled the Regiment to re-build its strength.

Chusan was evacuated in 1846, and the 98th embarked for Calcutta for its first Indian tour. After a few months in Calcutta the regiment marched some 360 miles up country to Dinapore. In 1848 the 98th marched 600 miles to Meerut, but were only to stay a little while. With hostilities breaking out again with the Sikhs, who had previously been defeated in the Sutlej campaign of

China 1842 campaign medal awarded to "John Bannister 98th Regiment Foot".

1845-46, the 98th were ordered to the Punjab, and though not being involved in any of the major engagements of this second Sikh war, the flank companies provided an escort for the Governor General. At the same time the remainder of the 98th protected a large treasure convoy to Lahore. The 98th Foot's services was recognised with the award of the battle honour, PUNJAUB 1849.

The annexation of the Punjab on the conclusion of this war brought the British for the first time into contact with the North-West Frontier and the warlike Pathan tribesmen, with whom the British were going to be in conflict for the next hundred years, off and on. Marching to Peshawar in 1849, the 98th were one of the first British regiments to serve on "the Frontier", and soon saw active service. The flank companies were included in a force under their former Commanding Officer, Sir Colin Campbell, later Field-Marshal Lord Clyde, and were sent to deal with the Afridis of the Kohat Pass region in 1850. This initial operation became the normal routine for such future operations. A quick and fierce engagement at the entrance to the Pass, the

Punjab campaign medal awarded to "Wm. Charles 98th Foot"

column then advanced up the Pass driving the Afridis from the hills on either side of the Pass. The 98th took their full share in this task. Then a salutary lesson was dealt out to the tribesmen with their principal village being burnt to the ground. This column then retired back down the Pass, being sniped and harried by the Afridis from the hills all the way.

The 98th Foot's detachment was extremely lucky to only have two casualties; the careful drill for 'picquetting the heights', which the British troops developed in future years, was at this time unknown to the 98th Foot. But the loss of men of the 98th Foot to disease was large even for those days. There were 1,164 deaths, none as a result of enemy action, with a further 176 invalided home, during the Regiment's nine years foreign service up to 1851. And although the 98th Foot received upwards of 300 volunteers from other regiments while at Dinapore, in the main the Regiment's losses were rectified by drafts from home.

Numbered buttons of the 98th Foot including mess waiters.

Three uneventful years preceded a move back to Calcutta in 1854. The march from Dagshai in the Punjab Hills was followed by boat to the River Ganges close to Meerut. The Regiment then left India for the Crimea, despite 120 men on detachment not being able to reunite with the Regiment on time. Half of these rejoined their comrades later on.

Disappointingly for the 98th, hopes of active service in the Crimea were diverted, and instead the next three years were spent in England, in the main at Sheffield and Weedon in Birmingham. It was from the latter that the 98th Foot formed a guard of honour and street lining detachments for the Prince Consort's Birmingham visit.

The Militia built the Regiment up again from its volunteers during the 98th's stay at Sheffield. An Irish sergeant within the Regiment bears witness to generous leave being allocated at the time - he was able to take a month's furlough at home annually.

The 98th embarked for India, this time without their families, towards the end of 1857, where the Mutiny had broken out. On landing at Karachi in January 1858, they were sent to Nowshera and Campbellpore, on the frontier between Peshawar and Rawalpindi which had to be guarded - so the Regiment saw no action with the Mutineers. A strong detachment of four companies of the 98th Foot were sent to join the Sittana Field Force shortly after their arrival, to engage and defeat the Khudu Khel tribe and the Hindustani Fanatics, who had attacked the British assistant commissioner, and had killed some of his escort.

The 98th Foot provided the British column element of the three columns which moved through a narrow pass to find the Khudu Khel's principal village of Chinglai abandoned, and the tribesmen concentrated on a ridge beyond. The 5th Punjab Infantry outflanked these and the 98th made a frontal attack, but the enemy succeeded in retiring, leaving a number of their dead behind. This engagement seemed to dispose of the threat of the Khudu Khel, as the entire force then concentrated against the Hindustani Fanatics stronghold Sittana, which was taken and destroyed without a great deal of trouble. Despatches in regard of this campaign make particular note of the 98th Foot's excellent work, especially with their Enfield rifles, covering the withdrawal of the picquets.

Lasting until 1866, this Indian tour, predominantly of the Punjab, was followed by another three years in England, and an inevitable split up, with detachments in Ireland in those troubled times for the province.

In 1871, while at Templemore in County Tipperary, the Commanding Officer and two companies rushed to Cashel, because the Tipperary Light Infantry Militia, embodied for training, had broken out of their barracks and attacked the local police station. Arriving in the evening the detachments put a guard on the barracks, and the following morning assisted the police to arrest the ringleaders, and put the rest of this militia unit on the train for Curragh where there was a large garrison. The following week this militia returned and

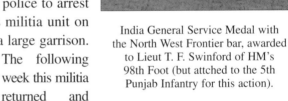

India General Service Medal with the North West Frontier bar, awarded to Lieut T. F. Swinford of HM's 98th Foot (but attched to the 5th Punjab Infantry for this action).

were disembodied under the 98th Foot's supervision.

The 64th Foot and the 98th Foot were now linked as a result of the Cardwell Reforms in 1873. Later in 1873, the 98th embarked for the West Indies, apparently a popular posting with the company commanders, with Regimental Headquarters in Barbados, and detachments in Jamaica, Trinidad and Demerara (and for a while at Nassau, Bahamas). By now 'Yellow Jack' (yellow fever) was a less serious threat, health being good in general. Perhaps, however, the West Indies was less popular than India, because on the 98th Foot's embarkation to Malta in 1875 they were asked to provide 100 volunteers for the 35th Foot, the succeeding regiment, and only 78 were forthcoming.

The Regiment was now armed with the new Martini-Henry fast-loading rifle. The ultimate event whilst in Malta was the presentation, in April 1876, by

Glengarry badge of the 98th Foot.

H.R.H. the Prince of Wales (King Edward VII) of new regimental colours. Replying to the Royal speech, the Commanding Officer, Colonel Lloyd, took the opportunity to mention that the previous 98th had been The Prince of Wales's. Taking the hint, and obviously impressed with what he saw, H.R.H. honoured the Regiment by bestowing on them the title "98th or Prince of Wales's Regiment of Foot" the following October.

In 1877 there was a renewed threat of war with Russia and all Mediterranean regiments were brought up to full strength, the 64th providing a draft of no less than 200 men for the 98th Foot. As these troops were disembarking in the Mediterranean, the men enlisted under Cardwell's 1870 scheme were embarking for home.

Though this Near Eastern crisis was defused with the Congress of Berlin (Disraeli's 'Peace with Honour'), war had now erupted in Afghanistan, and reinforcements, including the 98th Foot, were sent. Though not required in the field, they were garrisoned at Karachi, and again were badly affected by malaria resulting in a move to a 'health camp'. The sick were averaging around 60 a day, although things were better nine months later.

1881 saw the Cardwell Reforms carried out, the linked regiments now becoming amalgamated. The 64th Foot and the 98th Foot became the 1st and the 2nd Battalions of the Prince of Wales's (North Staffordshire) Regiment, and, at Whittington Barracks, Lichfield, a permanent Depot was established, along with the South Staffordshire Regiment. Previously, depots had consisted of training companies

98th Foot swagger stick.

attached to other regiments when the unit was overseas, or even earlier a depot battalion.

Included in the new regiment were two militia battalions, the 3rd and 4th, formerly the 2nd and 3rd King's Own Staffordshire Militia, which had been based on the Stafford and Newcastle-under-Lyme Militias respectively. The 2nd and 5th Staffordshire Rifle Volunteers became the 1st and 2nd Volunteer Battalions in 1883, with their headquarters at Stoke-on-Trent and Lichfield, though this was later moved to Burton-on-Trent.

These amalgamations were not as drastic as one might think, compared with those of eighty years later when two quite different regiments, the North and South Staffords were reduced to one. The two battalions, although officially adopting the same territorial title, wearing the same uniform, and with their individuals able to be cross posted, in practice still managed largely to keep their individual identities. A Battalion Order dated 25th February 1919 bears out the strong independent identity of the 2nd Battalion, The Prince of Wales's (North Staffordshire) Regiment, in that it still refers to itself as the XCVIII (98th Regt) which it had actually ceased to exist 38 years previously.

The Staffordshire Volunteer Artillery

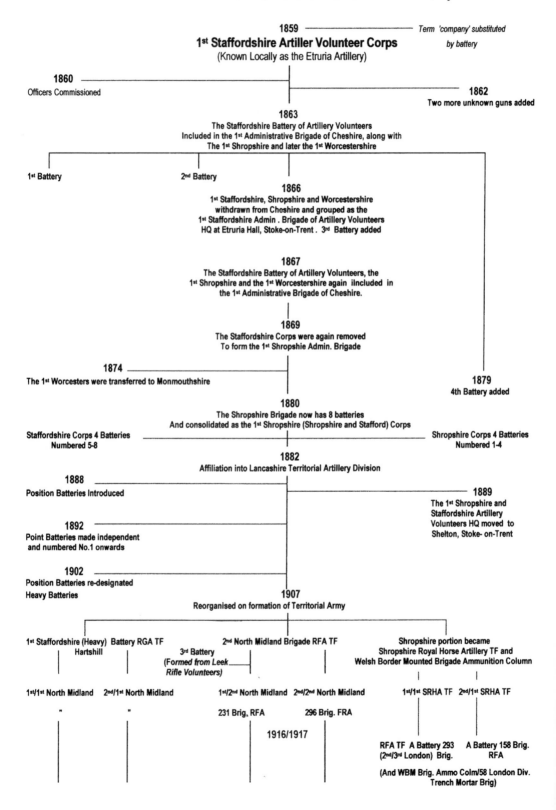

1859 ———————————————— *Term 'company' substituted*
1st Staffordshire Artiller Volunteer Corps   *by battery*
(Known Locally as the Etruria Artillery)

1860 ————
Officers Commissioned

1862
Two more unknown guns added

1863
The Staffordshire Battery of Artillery Volunteers
Included in the 1st Administrative Brigade of Cheshire, along with
The 1st Shropshire and later the 1st Worcestershire

1st Battery   2nd Battery

1866
1st Staffordshire, Shropshire and Worcestershire
withdrawn from Cheshire and grouped as the
1st Staffordshire Admin . Brigade of Artillery Volunteers
HQ at Etruria Hall, Stoke-on-Trent . 3rd Battery added

1867
The Staffordshire Battery of Artillery Volunteers, the
1st Shropshire and the 1st Worcestershire again iIncluded in
the 1st Administrative Brigade of Cheshire.

1869
The Staffordshire Corps were again removed
To form the 1st Shropshie Admin. Brigade

1874 ————
The 1st Worcesters were transferred to Monmouthshire

1879
4th Battery added

1880
The Shropshire Brigade now has 8 batteries
And consolidated as the 1st Shropshire (Shropshire and Stafford) Corps

Staffordshire Corps 4 Batteries ——————————————— Shropshire Corps 4 Batteries
Numbered 5-8   Numbered 1-4

1882
Affiliation into Lancashire Territorial Artillery Division

1888 ————
Position Batteries Introduced

1889
The 1st Shropshire and
Staffordshire Artillery
Volunteers HQ moved to
Shelton, Stoke- on-Trent

1892 ————
Point Batteries made independent
and numbered No.1 onwards

1902 ————
Position Batteries re-designated
Heavy Batteries

1907
Reorganised on formation of Territorial Army

1st Staffordshire (Heavy) Battery RGA TF   2nd North Midland Brigade RFA TF   Shropshire portion became
Hartshill   Shropshire Royal Horse Artillery TF and
3rd Battery   Welsh Border Mounted Brigade Ammunition Column
(Formed from Leek
Rifle Volunteers)

1st/1st North Midland   2nd/1st North Midland   1st/2nd North Midland   2nd/2nd North Midland   1st/1st SRHA TF   2nd/1st SRHA TF

"   "   231 Brig. RFA   296 Brig. FRA

1916/1917

RFA TF A Battery 293   A Battery 158 Brig.
(2nd/3rd London) Brig.   RFA

(And WBM Brig. Ammo Colm/58 London Div.
Trench Mortar Brig)

Seven
The History of The Staffordshire Volunteer Artillery from 1860 up until 1908, and the 2nd North Midland Brigade R.F.A. up until 1914

A letter from the Duke of Wellington, at the age of 77, to Sir John Burgoyne, in 1847, expressed the Duke's anxiety at the state of the home defences of Britain. The Duke was not in agreement with the opinion that was generally held by the British Government that the United Kingdom was safe from attack, and made strong representations that some sort of national defence force should be started. The government of the day were not in agreement with such a sizeable force being established. Furthermore there was a fear that these part-time amateur soldiers might interfere with recruiting for the regular army.

It was not until 1858, with the French 'invasion scare' resulting from the increasing animosity with the old enemy, that volunteers were again proposed by the British Government. On the 12th May, 1859, the War Office finally sanctioned the formation of volunteer corps. The County Lord Lieutenants commissioned officers, and organised oaths of allegiance and call-out.

In the time of call-out, volunteers were subject to military law, but also had to receive pay as per their

Wellington

regular counterparts. Though some finance to form and equip volunteers was obtained from public subscriptions, volunteers were often expected to provide their own uniforms, arms and equipment, subject to the approval of the Lord Lieutenant. All volunteers were exempt from the Militia ballot, but had to perform drill daily for eight days in every four months. A fortnight's notice of resignation was also required, and while on active service no volunteer could quit his corps.

The men of Stoke-on-Trent were no exception to the formation of volunteer rifle corps, holding a meeting at the Wedgwood Works in Stoke chaired by Mr John Greatbach, a local business man. At first Mr Wedgwood was asked to command the proposed rifle unit, but he felt that a younger man was required, suggesting Mr William Roden, who had recently moved into Etruria Hall, and was a working partner at Shelton Bar Iron works.

Mr Roden had other ideas, and instead of rifles decided the unit would be one of artillery. This was a popular suggestion and Mr Roden was elected Captain at the following meeting. Mr Roden also brought along proposed uniform samples to this meeting, and a uniform conforming to the current garrison artillery uniform appears to have been adopted; a blue uniform with white belts and a busby. Now that the uniform had been agreed upon, the NCOs were selected and enrolled along with the men at the same meeting:

Sgt Major: John Greatbach   Sgts: John Roberts, John Bromley, Will Simpson, Henry Cartledge

The uniforms for the unit were made by Enoch Jarvis, tailor, of Etruria. The unit's first piece of ordnance was a 32 pdr (supplied by the War Office). The first drill hall was the Schoolroom of Etruria village, and the unit's initial parade took place on Hall Fields.

1st Staffordshire (Etruscan) Artillery Volunteer Corps, c. 1860   (Many thanks to Maurice Holland).

The circular of 25th May 1859 made clear the government's expectations for their required standards of drill and discipline, and that the manning of batteries for coastal protection should be the volunteer artillery corps primary objective, being recruited from local men, married, with other business ties to a locality, or unfit for field service, but who could find the time to learn how to use such batteries.

The War Office circular of 13th July 1859, further made clear the government's views regarding necessary standards. The accompanying memorandum set out the establishment for all such corps. These were to comprise of not fewer than 50 or in excess of 80 effectives, and to include a captain, lieutenant and 2nd lieutenant. Any sub divisions were then to consist of no fewer than 30 effectives with a lieutenant and a 2nd lieutenant, as could sections of not fewer than 20 under a lieutenant. This memorandum also went on to settle the subject of precedence, with the various arms of the volunteer force in line with their regular counterparts. Artillery at the time of this memo ranked above rifles. The final precedence was as follows: Light Horse, Artillery, Engineers, Mounted Rifles and Rifles.

The initial freedom of choice in uniform led to a considerable variety of designs amongst the earliest corps, especially those with wealthy patronage who could afford more elaborate uniforms. Most corps adopted blue uniforms similar to those of the regular army Royal

Artillery, often embroidered with black or silver braid.

The precedence of a county corps was reflected by the number it was given by the Secretary of State for War. The Lord Lieutenant, on the application for the formation of a corps, would date it, and forward this offer to the War Office. Once satisfied that the proposed corps had satisfied all conditions required, The Secretaryof State for War would, in respect of the date of this application by the Lord Lieutenant, give the corps its number. The date of the letter from HM Queen Victoria informing the corps of the acceptance of their service, was considered as the official date of formation of these corps. As soon as possible after this acceptance the gazetting of the officers was conducted.

On the 18th December, 1860, the officers of the first Staffordshire Artillery Volunteer Corps, more commonly known (certainly locally) as 'The Etruria Artillery', were given commissions, and this date acts as the unit's official 'birthday'. The strength of the unit at this time is recorded as 80. (The Staffordshire Volunteer Artillery were low in the order of seniority No. 58 of 64 corps, being fairly late in applying for acceptance of their service). The first officers were:

Capt: W.S. Roden, Lt: M. Brown, 2nd Lt: J.B. Blackstone, Chaplain Rev C.P. Villiers (Etruria Church)

The Government of the time soon looked at the question of volunteer uniforms in general, a report in January 1860 recommending patterns and colours of uniforms. The pattern recommended was the same as that for the Rifle Volunteers but of blue cloth with scarlet piping and black belts - though many corps preferred to wear white waist and pouch belts. The Austrian knot on the cuff of the tunic sleeve was adopted as the distinguishing mark of most volunteer corps, prior to 1878 this being in black, white or silver on most uniforms.

In 1861, the first Volunteer Regulations emphasised no gold lace should be worn by volunteers, being reserved as a distinguishing mark for regular artillery. From the very beginning, silver lace, silver or silver plated badges and buttons for officers and white metal badges and buttons of other ranks were worn by artillery volunteers, continuing right up until 1908.

The batteries' strength increased when two more unknown types of guns were supplied to the First Staffordshire Artillery Volunteer Corps in 1862. Along with these came Sergeant Major Dan Ricards (late of the RHA), who was destined to bring the first Staffordshire Artillery Volunteer Corps to a high state of efficiency in time to come.

Life was at a steady pace for the First Staffordshire Artillery Volunteer Corps, under the instruction of Sergeant Major Ricards. The normal position for the corps guns was in front of the hall on a platform, and the guns would have been on

Sergeant of the 1st Staffordshire (Etruscan) Artillery Volunteer Corps, c 1861 - (Many thanks to Peter Lead).

garrison type carriages. Etruria Hall had a large woodland park in those days, and a place known as Shady Grove was the First Staffordshire Artillery Volunteer Corps' favourite drill ground. Sergeant Major Ricards lived in the armoury cottages of the hall with his wife and the cottages doubled as headquarters for the Volunteer Corps.

In 1863 the Staffordshire Battery of Artillery Volunteers was included in the 1st Administrative Brigade of Cheshire. In addition the 1st Shropshire and later the 1st Worcestershire were also attached to this brigade. In 1863 Volunteer Regulations ordered all the corps in an admin. battalion to dress alike, the material for uniforms to be issued at cost price from the Army Clothing Depot thus ensuring all artillery volunteer corps adopted the basic uniform patterns worn by the Royal Artillery. A variety of types of head dress was worn by the artillery volunteers, especially those formed early on. Some wore 'pill box' forage caps, others wore peaked caps or shakos, similar in design to those worn by regular infantry regiments between 1855-1861

The First Staffordshire Artillery Volunteer Corps continued to grow; in 1863 the Corps had increased to 2 batteries, and in 1866 a 3rd battery was formed, with a 4th battery being added in 1879. At the annual review at Stafford Common in 1864, the First Staffordshire Artillery Volunteer Corps are recorded as having "2 breach loading guns".

The administrative brigades mainly catered for rural corps e.g. 1st Staffordshire Admin. Brigade. In 1866 the 1st Staffordshire, Shropshire and Worcestershire were withdrawn from Cheshire and grouped as the 1st Staffordshire Admin. Brigade of Artillery Volunteers, with headquarters at Etruria Hall, and their own staff. Such administrative brigades were able to remain financially independent and distinct, and also allowed to keep their allotted county numbers. However the Staffordshire Brigade was short lived and by October, 1867 the three corps were again shown as part of the 1st Cheshire.

As an artillery unit, the First Staffordshire Artillery Volunteer Corps was in great demand on ceremonial occasions. Seven shots from each gun were fired on the funeral day of the Prince Consort. The Corps (along with all the other volunteer units of Stoke-on-Trent) took part in the parade at the unveiling of the statue of Josiah Wedgwood, outside Stoke Station, and fired a salute using two 12 pdr guns, when the Prince of Wales laid the foundation Stone for the North Staffs Royal Infirmary on the 16th December 1869.

Corps were designated in the first regulations for volunteers in 1861, additionally special titles were allowed. These regulations also stipulated on the disbandment or absorption of a corp into a senior one, its number was to stay vacant.

Other rank's helmet plate of the 1st Staffordshire Artillery Volunteer Corps.

Artillery Volunteers at Hanley.   *Courtesy of Barbara Hobson.*

In the regular army, the term 'company' was substituted by 'battery', by the Royal Artillery Regimental Order of 1st April 1859 which became effective after 1st July, 1859. The volunteers were to follow in due course with the term company absent from the Monthly Army List after March, 1860. Most corps had adopted the busby, as worn by the Royal Artillery, to wear with full dress at least by the mid 1860s.

Early in 1869, at Shoeburyness Artillery competition, two detachments of the First Staffordshire Artillery Volunteer Corps won the first consolation prize, and 11 men won the Elkington Prize.

In 1869 the corps were removed, this time to form the 1st Shropshire Admin. Brigade whose commanding officer was gazetted on the 15th May.

In 1870 the First Staffordshire Artillery Volunteer Corps were in Wolverhampton at the unveiling of the Albert statue. Unfortunately, one of the first Corps' gunners lost his arm in an accident. Queen Victoria personally directed that this gunner should receive a pension.

Another invalid was Sergeant Major Ricards, who suffered a heart attack when moving one of the guns and was immediately retired, taking the job of caretaker at Etruria Hall.

The officers of the First Staffordshire Artillery Volunteer Corps were recorded in 1871:

Lt Col: W.S. Roden	Maj. M. Brown	Capts: J. Strick, W. Bull
1st Lt: W. Acton	Adj: Capt Plunkett RA	Hon Qmr: H. Cartledge
Hon Asst. Surg: W.D. Spanton		

Total Strength 240

Col. Roden was at this time the mayor of Stoke-on-Trent, and later became its MP. Shortly after the list was taken, former Seargeant Major Ricards died at the age of 47. A large number of the First Staffordshire Artillery Volunteer Corps attended his funeral in Conway.

The 1st Worcesters were transferred to Monmouthshire in 1874. The Volunteer Regulations of 1878 were the initial instance where obligatory distinctive marks on uniforms were required to distinguish Volunteers from other branches of the Army; the Artillery Volunteers were ordered to wear scarlet Austrian knots on their tunics, scarlet bands and buttons on forage caps of all other ranks, whilst regulars wore these in yellow and the militia in white.

By 1880 home service blue cloth helmets were used by most corps, though some corps continued to wear the busby right up until 1908. The strength of the Shropshire Brigade stood at eight batteries by 1880. In this year the First Staffordshire Artillery Volunteer Corps was recorded as follows:

Hon Col: W.S. Roden	Lt Col: J. Strick	Maj: G.D. Harrison
Capts: J. West-Jones, H. Woolner, W. Thomson, H. Robinson		
Lts: G. Westhead, R. Topham Qmr: A. Jones		Act Chaplain: Rev. Bond
Adjutant: Capt. W.B. Hoggan RA		

Total Strength 304

The Shropshire and Staffordshire Corps consisted of four batteries each. In counties where there were insufficient corps for a brigade, these volunteer corps could join one of their neighbours. During 1880 the recommendations of the 1878 committee of the Parliamentary Under Secretary of State, Viscount Bury, were carried out and all remaining administrative units were consolidated. The corps, within each brigade, lost their independent status, and instead became numbered batteries of these new corps. This happened in May 1880, in Staffordshire and Shropshire, with the brigade consolidated as the 1st Shropshire (Shropshire and Stafford) Corps, the Staffords providing Nos. 5-8 Batteries at Etruria. In August of this year the corps were redesignated as the 1st Shropshire and Staffordshire Artillery Volunteers.

In 1881 Col. Roden died, and by now the old armoury cottages and the rolling parkland had been swallowed up by the ever increasing Shelton steelworks. The armoury cottages were finally demolished at the beginning of the 20th century.

In 1882 the Artillery Volunteer Corps became affiliated to nine of the eleven Territorial Divisions of Artillery formed that year. The 1st Shropshire and Staffordshire Artillery Volunteers were organised into the Lancashire Division along with the 1st to 8th Lancashire, 1st Cheshire and Caernarvon and the 9th Lancashire.

Because of the freedom given initially to the artillery volunteers in the way of uniform, many units wore badges and insignia on head dress items, sabretaches, pouches, waistbelt clasps, cross belts and buttons, distinctive to their own corp, frequently but not always, bearing the corps name or title.

In May 1888, position batteries were introduced to volunteer artillery. These batteries were intended to provide elements of semi-mobile field artillery to work with the infantry brigades, and were formed from troops of two of the existing garrison batteries. In 1889 the 1st Shropshire and Staffordshire Artillery Volunteers headquarters moved to Shelton, Stoke on Trent and in 1890 the corps were organised into four position batteries.

The manning of the position batteries by members of garrison companies led to a great

293 Q.M.S. John Nixon and members of his family on receipt of his
Volunteer Long Service Medal (34 years) April 1895 *(Many thanks to Maurice Holland).*

46th North Midland Division RGA (T.F.)
brass shoulder title.

Staffordshire Brigade RFA (T.F.)
brass shoulder title.

deal of confusion. In 1892 these were made independent and numbered from No. 1 onwards. Remaining garrison companies were then numbered on from the position batteries. Position batteries were then redesignated as Heavy Batteries by Army Order 120 of May 1902. As with the 1st Shropshire and Staffordshire Artillery Volunteers, where the corps consisted completely of these position/heavy batteries the style ('Position Artillery'/'Heavy Artillery') was added to the Army List, without becoming part of their title.

Under the Territorial and Reserve Forces Act of 1907, the Volunteer Force ceased to exist on the 31st

March, 1908. 1st April 1908 saw the Territorial Force born and the old volunteers invited to join. This change was not popular with its reorganisation, and in some cases disbandment, of many of the existing corps. The new force was soon

Officer's bronze collar dog of the Staffordshire Brigade RFA (T.F.).

18 pdr. fuse, shell-head and case of 1st World War vintage, as was used by the 46th North Midland Division RFA (T.F.).

established, however, with many of the former volunteer units transferring en masse.

On the transfer of the volunteers into the Territorial Force, the Staffordshire portion of the corps became the 2nd North Midland Brigade R.F.A, 1st and 2nd Batteries, while the Shropshire components formed the Shropshire Battery, R.H.A. and the Welsh Border Mounted Brigade Ammunition Column.

The 3rd Battery, on the formation of the Territorial Force, was raised from the Leek Rifle Volunteers commanded by Major W.F Challinor, with Lieuts Ward and Nicholson. From the total company strength of 120 of all ranks of the former Leek Rifle Volunteers, only 53 joined the battery, along with 70 new recruits, making a peacetime establishment of 145 all ranks.

This new 3rd Battery, though under strength, was composed of men from Leek and the local area. The 3rd Battery, like the townspeople, was a close knit community in the North-eastern part of Staffordshire. These new Territorials now had to master the field gun and the necessary four legged friends, of which they were to have 78. Their initial issue weapons were four 15 pdr, Boer War vintage, breech-loader field guns, that became obsolete at the introduction of the 18 pdr. quick firer in 1906.

These 15 pdr. breech loaders were being converted to quick firers, being re-designated 15 pdr. breech loader conversions, to try to improve them to the current standards. There resulted an unwieldy beast, with a large steel shroud that overshadowed the barrel and the recoil mechanism and that gave a most peculiar appearence. Furthermore propellant charge and shell were separate unlike the 18 pdr. shell and cartridge.

At a later date their 15 pdr. breach loader field guns were to be exchanged for these 15 pdr. breach loader conversion field guns. These were the weapons the 46th North Midland Division, Royal Field Artillery, Territorial Force would take with them to France in 1915 on their entry into the Great War, but they were soon replaced by 18 pdrs.

Gunner Wilding, North Midland RFA (T.F.) based at Shelton Barracks *(Many thanks to Peter Lead).*

The NCO's and Warrant Officers of the RFA (T.F.) 46th North Midland Division "A" and "B" Shelton; "C" Leek Batteries 1914. *(Many thanks to Maurice Holland).*

A soldier of the 80th Foot, recently returned from the Zulu War. This is just prior to the amalgamation of the 38th and 80th Foot to form the 1st and 2nd Battalion, South Staffordshire Regiment.

A very rare Victorian 1st V.B. blue cloth helmet and sergeant's tunic.

Eight
The History of The 1st and 2nd Battalions of the South Staffordshire Regiment from 1882 up until 1914

In 1881 foot regiments lost their old numbers, in most cases taking the name of the county of their origin. These infantry regiments were reorganised into two battalion regiments with territorial titles and permanent depots within the recruitment area. The 38th Foot (the 1st Staffordshire Regiment) and the 80th Foot (Staffordshire Volunteers) became the 1st and 2nd Battalions, The South Staffordshire Regiment. (The militia regiments were also to take county titles and in Staffordshire became the 3rd and 4th Battalions, while the Rifle Volunteers were ultimately to become the 1 Voluntary Brigade and 2 V.B. The South Staffordshire Regiment became the 5 Bn South Staffordshire Regiment in 1908, and the 3rd V.B. of the South Staffordshire Regiment became the 6th Bn South Staffordshire Regiment in 1908).

Other reforms had also taken place. Since 1871 officers were no longer able to purchase their commissions (a system that had been held in disrepute since before the Crimean War), and men were enlisted for a limited period followed by a time on the reserve. The idea was for one battalion of a regiment to serve at home, providing drafts for the other battalion of the regiment on foreign service, though this was not always the case in reality, but it did at least allow a soldier to spend some of his time soldiering at home. However, many who had enlisted for seven years spent as much as six of these years on service abroad.

It was not very long before the newly named 1st Battalion, The South Staffordshire Regiment had a chance of active service, when they were sent to Egypt in 1882. Egypt was at the time still nominally a Turkish possession, but Turkey's own troubles, and her notorious inefficiency and corruption, made her control very lax. Arabi Pasha, an army leader in Egypt, led a rebellion, and typical of other such 'mutinies', it started off with a religious massacre - this time of a large number of inoffensive Christians, mostly Greeks. For the defence of the Suez Canal, and humanitarian reasons, Great Britain could not stand aside, and so intervened. Britain's role as international policeman had the usual problems; foreign powers screamed for Britain's help if their trade or nationals were threatened, but then invariably stabbed Britain in the back by criticising any action taken.

The 1st South Staffords landed in Alexandria just after its bombardment by the Royal Navy and they were the first troops ashore. They were carrying their colours - this was to be the last time this was done by a British regiment on operations. They soon discovered that a large Egyptian army was only about 12 miles away, and a battle imminent. However, the Egyptian army declined to attack Alexandria; murdering Greek citizens was much safer than attacking trained soldiers who were spoiling for a fight.

With reinforcements arrived, Alexandria's garrison advanced on the rebels, more to distract their attention from the main British forces that were landing elsewhere, than to make a serious attack on the rebellious Egyptian army. This was very successful and enabled Sir Garnet Wolseley (who had served with the 80th) to defeat Arabi Pasha heavily at the battle of Tel-el-Kebir, and restore order. The 1st South Staffords had to be content with a few outpost skirmishes around Alexandria.

For their part, the South Staffordshire Regiment was awarded the battle honour, EGYPT 1882, to add to their long list of battle honours.

The 1st South Staffords in the Egyptian Campaign (Rob Chapman, Flintlock Publishing).

After a brief stay in Malta, the 1st South Staffords re-embarked for Egypt and then sent to the Sudan. This huge unhappy country, lying to the south of Egypt, had been under the control of Egypt, who mismanaged this with the usual corruptness of the area at this time. A well-known British officer, General Gordon, had been sent to Khartoum on a semi-official mission as Governor-General and was soon besieged by the Mahdi, who was leading an uprising. General Gordon refused to leave and hand over Khartoum to the Mahdi, and the public outcry in Britain forced the reluctant British Government to take action.

Two columns were despatched to relieve General Gordon in Khartoum, the 1st South Staffords heading the column advancing up the Nile, in turn with the Black Watch. To move a large, poorly-equipped force up an unknown river, in a tropical climate, to meet a hostile opponent, is, at best, a difficult task. The troops moved up the Nile in small boats against the current and in the blazing sun. When the sails could be used the boats would often run aground and have to be unloaded to get past the rapids. Food was in short supply forcing the leading units to draw rations from the reserve - and the unfortunate reserve units had to live off the country. The men of the 1st South Staffords must have been thankful to be in some form of tropical kit, even though it was buttoned to the neck and tightly fitting.

Unhappily, the relief arrived too late; Khartoum had fallen and General Gordon had died a hero's death. But he was soon to be avenged. Encouraged by their success at Khartoum, the Arabs advanced to meet the British force, but these were themselves spoiling for a fight to avenge General Gordon. The battle was at Kirbekan and the strong enemy force was soundly beaten, with great slaughter, by the 1st South Staffords and the Black Watch. British casualties were not heavy, but the General Officer Commanding and the Commanding Officers, of both the 1st South Staffords and the Black Watch, were killed in the fighting.

It is interesting to note that this was the last time that the South Staffordshire Regiment wore red in action, and that the men were ordered by their C.O., Colonel Eyre, to wear their

An original and contemporary print of the *"1st South Staffords pushing forward at the Hannek Cataract"* whilst advancing up the Nile.

The Egypt and Khedive's Star of Pte. A. Wall.

best clothes for the battle! Colonel Eyre had risen from a private soldier in the 38th to command the Regiment. This was also the final time that colours were carried on active service.

Early on during the battle, an orderly of the 1st South Staffords, while carrying a message, was attacked by an Arab. The Arab missed with his throwing spear and then decided to charge with his big knife. The orderly came to the 'on guard', but the Arab grabbed and held onto the orderly's bayonet. This somewhat flummoxed the orderly, as this manoeuvre was not in his drill book, and for a short while it was a question as to who would succeed in getting the rifle. The Englishman finally resolved this question by suddenly firing his rifle. The Arab was shot dead and departed to Paradise. When this orderly was congratulated by an officer who had observed the entire affair, he sheepishly grinned, *"Well, sir, I forgot if I had loaded my rifle - I did feel a fool!*

Most of the enemy were killed by the bayonet in the battle. The first of the two battle honours awarded are shared only with the Black Watch. Kitchener finally destroyed the Mahdi's army at Omdurman 14 years later. The South Staffordshire Regiment was awarded the battle honours, KIRBEKAN 1885 and NILE 1884-1885.

The 1st South Staffords returned to Egypt and then on to Gibraltar. Three years later they were back in Egypt, where for the first time they met the 2nd South Staffords. During the intervening three years in South-west Ireland, they had had many an unpleasant duty to perform amidst the unrest of the 1880s. It had been the usual policing work, with the splitting up of the Battalion into small detachments. Whilst employed in this unpleasant role the old 80th had become the 2nd Battalion, The South Staffordshire Regiment. It must have come as a welcome relief to embark for home and Lichfield.

Back in England, the 2nd South Staffords still had to find detachments for strike duties, the last in Manchester

A Victorian officer's tunic and blue cloth helmet.

A Victorian South Staffords officer's belt buckle.

A Victorian 1st V.B., 2nd V.B., 3rd V.B. and officer's 1st V.B. Glengarry badges.

in 1884. Their next posting was to Plymouth - always a favourite with the former 80th Regiment. When the 2nd North Staffords joined the 2nd South Staffords they were treated very hospitably and entertained by their fellow 'Countymen'. Some confusion resulted from the North Staffords being in the South Barracks and the South Staffords being in the North Barracks. The 2nd South Staffords now moved to Curragh for two years, then on to Egypt via Aldershot, where the 1st and 2nd South Staffords now also met for the first time, though 100 years earlier the 38th and 80th foot had served alongside each other in Flanders during the Napoleonic War.

Two quiet years later the 2nd South Staffords were posted to Southern India, where they saw action against the Moplahs, averting a prolonged campaign by drastic action in their first engagement. They had service in Burma for a while, but they were back in India by the end of the century.

Ten years were now spent in Ireland and England and under the linked battalion system, the 2nd South Staffords provided drafts of men for the 1st South Staffords who were serving abroad. This new arrangement ensured that the different battalions had approximately an equal amount of service at home and overseas, a welcome change to both South Staffs Battalions as previously most of their service had been abroad.

Therefore, as the 2nd South Staffords went to Egypt, the 1st South Staffords came back home. It had been an eventful time - five major campaigns, innumerable small ones and three shipwrecks made a record of which any unit might be proud. These "plucky dogs", as Sir Harry Smith called the 80th, had indeed served their country well.

In 1894 the 1st South Staffords were stationed in Lichfield for the first time in over 100 years. After four years in their home station and Aldershot, they embarked for Ireland, but not for long. Trouble was brewing again in South Africa . Bad feelings between the Dutch settlers, the Boers, and the British colonists had come to a head, and war was declared by Great Britain on the Boer Republics.

The 1st South Staffords were ordered from Ireland to Gibraltar and then found themselves ordered back to England to mobilise. They left England in March 1900 and stopped at St. Vincent in the Cape Verde Islands to coal. Unfortunately, there was a case of measles on board ship and they were immediately placed in quarantine. No coolies were allowed on board, but the 1st South Staffords re-coaled the ship themselves in the very quick time of two days.

The 1st South Staffords joined the 8th Division on their arrival in South Africa. The 8th Division were nicknamed, with very good reason, the "Starving Eighth". Perpetually ill-equipped and underfed, the battalion never the less marched magnificently until the tracks showed the bloody imprints of their feet, and they fought gallantly. In view of this marching it was easy to raise volunteers for the mounted infantry. Each infantry unit raised at least one company, and often more than this, and these rendered yeoman service.

One of the 1st South Staffords' mounted infantry companies took part in the last action of the war. During the latter part of the Boer War there were more skirmishes than battles. The long lines of block-houses, usually covering the railways, did much to reduce the marching required.

The Militia battalions of both the South Staffordshire and the Prince of Wales's (North

An other ranks 3rd V.B. Victorian blue cloth helmet plate,
and an other ranks 2nd V.B. Edwardian blue cloth helmet plate.

A Victorian regular and 1st V.B. cap badge along with a Victorian sweet heart brooch
and Boer War period bordered brass shoulder title.

Staffordshire Regiment) served in the Boer War and rendered much useful work in garrison duties, looking after prisoners and supplying men to the regular battalions; they saw a considerable amount of action. It is also interesting to note that a service company from the South Staffordshire Regiment Volunteers (and also from the Prince of Wales's, North Staffordshire Regiment), took an active part in the Boer War. The Boer War transformed the young, raw officers and soldiers into seasoned veterans and these would become the leaders in the much greater war to come little over a decade later.

The 1st South Staffords losses in the war, as usual, were chiefly through disease, three times as many being killed by enteric fever (typhoid) than by enemy action, despite the untiring efforts of the Army Medical Service. The 1st South Staffords were more fortunate than most other units. Progress in medical science would help prevent such widespread sickness in the Great War. Yet another battle honour, SOUTH AFRICA 1900-1902, was awarded to the South Staffordshire Regiment and placed on their colours.

The 1st South Staffords
throughout the Boer War
(Rob Chapman
Flintlock Publishing).

An other ranks Victorian Volunteer
Battalion belt and buckle.

In 1900 the 2nd South Staffords were serving in India. In 1906 new colours were presented to the Regiment by the Prince of Wales, later to become King George V. Speaking to the 2nd South Staffords he said:

"Meeting here to perform this ceremony on Indian soil we are reminded that during the 112 years that have elapsed since your Battalion was raised, some of its most brilliant services have been achieved in this portion of the British Empire.

With regard to its gallant conduct at Ferozashah in 1845, Lord Hardinge, the then Governor-General of India, described it as "that Regiment that has earned immortal fame in the annals of the British Army", and not only on the field of battle has your Regiment gained renown, for no less than three times did it suffer shipwreck in Eastern waters.

The 1st South Staffords were at Alexandria, in Egypt, in 1882. This picture shows the Highlanders at Tel-el-Kebir, near Alexandria, in 1882.

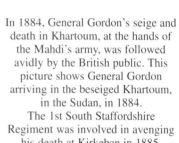

In 1884, General Gordon's seige and death in Khartoum, at the hands of the Mahdi's army, was followed avidly by the British public. This picture shows General Gordon arriving in the beseiged Khartoum, in the Sudan, in 1884.
The 1st South Staffordshire Regiment was involved in avenging his death at Kirkeban in 1885.

A Victorian Boer War chocolate tin and Queen's, and King's South Africa medal pair to Pte. Turner of the South Staffs Regiment.

We know there is no greater test of the discipline of a Regiment than under such terrible experiences, and the conduct of the 80th Regiment in the last disaster of this nature in 1844, was brought to the notice of Queen Victoria, and commended in a General Order by the Governor-General of India.

It is indeed a grand tradition which surrounds the Colours of your Regiment, a tradition created by those who, in days gone by, fought and fell in their defence.

I feel sure they will inspire the same spirit of loyalty to your King, your Country and your Regiment, and that, if needs be, you will, like your predecessors, do and die in the defence of these sentiments. With such convictions I have great pleasure in entrusting to your keeping these consecrated Colours".

Even though this chapter is of the South Staffordshire Regiment between 1882 and 1914, I feel these words should be recorded here. It is also poignant if it is remembered that they would come true for many of the listeners, who would die in France and Flanders.

In his reply the Commanding Officer emphasised the close connection between the 2nd South Staffords and Staffordshire.

The following year, 1907, the 2nd South Staffords left India, receiving a glowing testimonial from the Chief of Police on their conduct, and they sailed for Pretoria in South Africa. In 1911 the 2nd South Staffords were posted back to Lichfield, but from there on to the North of England, after depositing their old colours in Lichfield Cathedral. Following this they performed guard duties at Windsor Castle and service at Rugby.

They moved back down to Aldershot in 1913. A year later they moved to France as one of the first battalions of the British Expeditionary Force in the 1914-1918 War.

The 1st South Staffords were to remain in South Africa after the Boer War until 1904,

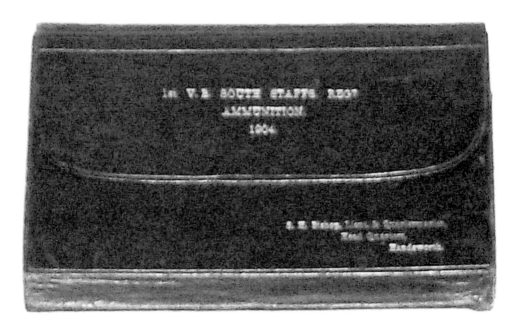

A Victorian leather 'ammo' returns pouch of the 1st V.B.

from whence they embarked for Ireland. They were posted to Borden Camp near Aldershot in 1906, and two years later to Davenport. Fom here they embarked for Gibraltar, passing the outward 2nd South Staffords on their way home in the Bay of Biscay. Unusually the weather must have been very calm with the two troop ships passing within 200 yards of each other, and with both battalions cheering each other enthusiastically.

A short time after their arrival in Gibraltar it was the 1st South Staffords turn to receive colours from King George V. In presenting them His Majesty said:

"I am very glad to present to you new colours, and thus to be brought into closer contact with a Battalion whose good work for the British Empire has, I think, hardly a parallel in our military history.

By your continuous service of nearly 60 consecutive years in the West Indies you enjoy a distinction which is unique in the Army. Be proud of it, and do not mistake its significance. The West Indies in those days were the most valuable possessions in the world. The climate was deadly; and there was a good deal more petty fighting to be done than you are probably aware of. The work then required of you was much the same on a small scale, as that now required of the entire Army in every quarter of the globe. You were the first to enter upon that heavy task, and since then you have well continued it. North America, Central America, South America, North Africa, South Africa, the Plains of India and the Mountains of India; Northern Europe and Southern Europe; Holland, the Peninsula and the Crimea; no part of the world has come amiss to you, and you have spent abroad three-quarters of the two centuries of your Regimental life, always and unchangeably with honour.

A Regiment's Colours no longer go into action; but they do not on that account lose their old importance. A consecrated Colour is a sacred emblem, to be venerated and treasured as a token of the trust to your Sovereign and your Country in you.

It is also something more. It is the outward and visible sign of a Regiment's traditions. You have the old staves which first went under fire at Roleia, and since then have been carried through many actions and many Campaigns.

Remembering the glorious traditions of the Regiment, I commit these new Colours with confidence to your keeping".

In his reply the Commanding Officer of the 1st South Staffords assured His Majesty of the pride and appreciation, not only of those present, but also of future men of the Regiment. He mentioned the close connection between the Regiment and its County of Staffordshire.

In writing about the ceremony, the Hon. John Fortescue, a very celebrated Army historian said:

"The 38th, albeit a Corps of which the newspapers, and as a natural consequence, the public, knows nothing, has one of the most remarkable records of service in the Army........ one could not help reflecting that if this Regiment wore the kilt the whole British Empire would ring with its fame".

The 1st South Staffords were again in South Africa in 1914, at the beginning of the 1914-1918 War.

A group of other ranks regular and volunteer, Queen's and King's crown blue cloth helmet plates.

An officer's and other ranks, 1st Volunteer Battalion, Glengarry badges and a 2nd Volunteer Battalion other ranks Glengarry badge.

Bottom: An officer's, sword belt buckle.

Nine
The History of The Prince of Wales's
(North Staffordshire) Regiment from 1881 up until 1914

The former 98th, now the 2nd Battalion the Prince of Wales's (North Staffordshire) Regiment, was the first to see action as North Staffords. A fresh piece of territory had been taken as a result of the Afghan war, north of Quetta, but was constantly raided by the little-known Zhob Valley inhabitants. In September 1884 the British decided to go and sort them out with an especially assembled Zhob Field Force. The 2nd Battalion North Staffords was the biggest element of the three British regiments concerned.

Initially things went badly, sickness picked up in Quetta causing fifty men to be sent back after the third day's march. Now picking up after the initial sickness, the remainder of the 2nd Battalion had cleared the country up to the Zhob Valley itself, after some initial operations that were unopposed. The British element of the flying column were then elected to go into and capture the Zhobi's principal village. Though accomplished again without opposition, the enemy was observed gathering a few miles away on a ridge. To disperse this hostile gathering three companies of the North Staffords, the 4th Punjab Infantry and two other Indian regiments, along with a Mountain Battery, were despatched.

This force found themselves facing the enemy's position, alongside a small pass, after a night approach march. A company of the Staffords protected the artillery when they opened fire from the centre, the other two companies of the Staffords "took to the hills in splendid style" on the left, whilst the Punjabis, advancing first, had some hand-to-hand fighting and took some casualties. The Zhobis retreated prior to the arrival of the Staffords, leaving about 100 dead behind them. This engagement, which apparently lasted about

How the 2nd Battalion, The Prince of Wales's (North Staffordshire) Regiment would have looked in dress uniform from a contemporary print.

two hours, was the only serious action fought in the campaign.

A detachment of Staffords was in another small column sent to sort out a recalcitant headman, but without a fight in this case, and all the enemy's forts were blown up. The 2nd

Battalion had marched approximately 700 miles, and returned to base with the knowledge of a task, although not spectacular, well done. It was remarkably similar to the operation carried out by the Sittana Field Force 25 years previously. A Zhobi sheep was chosen as a trophy of the campaign by the 2nd Battalion. This became a regimental mascot, before falling down a well and drowning at Devonport five years later.

A cholera epidemic swept through the Regiment shortly after the Zhob Valley campaign.   After a year in the Central Provinces, the Regiment embarked for a two-year tour in Aden, but it was difficult keeping the troops occupied in this unpopular posting. In contrast, the officers benefited and enjoyed big game shooting in Somaliland.

The 2nd Battalion arrived back in Devonport, in 1888, for three years, and the following two changes of station embarked for Ireland in 1893. A stay at Newry in County Down followed two years in Dublin. Only one permanent detachment was required of the 2nd Battalion whilst at Newry showing how the times had changed in Ireland just a few years.

In 1881 the 64th was in Templemore in Ireland when they became the 1st Battalion the Prince of Wales's (North Staffordshire) Regiment.   Their traditional old black facings were now replaced by the universal

A 2nd Volunteer Battalion officer's blue cloth helmet.

white of English regiments of the line - including the 98th (now the 2nd Battalion the Prince of Wales's (North Staffordshire) Regiment). The 1st Battalion seems to have been under strength accepting a draft of 63 recruits from the 2nd South Staffs in 1882, under the Army Act clause allowing the compulsory transfer of men with less than three months service.

The 1st Battalion embarked for Barbados in 1886 for two years with detachments in Trinidad and Jamaica. From there they went to the Natal, and a place called Pietermaritzburg. Whilst there a number of small detachments were found for Zululand, and from 1888 a detachment for Mauritius too. There was some serious rioting in Port Louis in Mauritius in 1889, from which the detachment concerned emerged with enormous credit.

In 1888 there were 80 district and 34 regimental court-martials, regimental discipline being low in South Africa. The dominant reason was insubordination, possibly due to inexperienced NCOs of the short service system that the 'old sweats' did not take to, and the Battalion was split. In those days drunkenness was a problem, to such an extent that a special order was issued to prevent men who had been to the bar in the station from sleeping it off on the railway tracks. Though the next year saw the figures for insubordination fall dramatically,

77 cases of desertion occurred, attributed to the attraction of the goldfields. One presumes the deserters incorporated the majority of the insubordinate soldiers of the previous year.

Leaving a detachment in Cape Town, the 1st Battalion embarked for Mauritius for three years in 1890. A devastating hurricane struck the island whilst the Regiment was there, which caused a great many civilian casualties. The soldiers helped in repairing damage and rescuing trapped victims, earning great praise from all concerned.

They moved to Malta from Mauritius, and then to Cairo. H.R.H the Duke of Cambridge presented the first colours, as North Staffords, to the 1st Battalion there. The reconquest of the Sudan was decided upon, abandoned after the fall of Khartoum in 1885. At last the Regiment would get to see some active service. The initial phase was to be the occupation of the northern province of Dongola, as a stepping stone and base for the main operation, which would take place two years afterwards. Under the command of Lord Kitchener, Egyptian Army troops were now trained and led by British officers of the 1st North Staffords.

As usual, logistics proved to be the major obstacle. Lord Kitchener had to rely on the seasonal River Nile whose many cataracts hindered easy navigation. A railway led to the forward outpost of Wadi Halfa, but beyond this was only the abandoned 33 mile track laid by Lord Wolseley in 1884, which led to Sarras and Dongola, 200 miles away from Wadi Halfa.

By March 1896 Lord Kitchener made his first assault, with part of his force seizing Akaisha 75 miles south of Wadi Halfa, unopposed. Simultaneously the North Staffords were ordered to Wadi Halfa, where they had been preceded by a Maxim gun detachment of twelve men and an officer attached to the Egyptian army. For three tedious, hot, boring and fly infested months, the Regiment remained at Wadi Halfa, while logistical arrangements for their advance were organised. The main occupation was fishing in the Nile with improvised hooks and cotton lines. The officers also read to the men from the few available books, to help kill the time. Things were livened up when the wives of the Egyptian troops, who had gone forward, became so infuriated by the rising prices in the nearby village that they sacked the bazaar and demanded to be sent forward alongside their husbands to fight.

The Egyptian army, incorporating the Maxim detachment, now saw action. At Firket, close to Akaisha, 3,000 Dervishes had appeared. The Egyptian troops moved out to meet them at night, the infantry advancing frontally, whilst the cavalry performed a turning manoeuvre. The Dervishes were routed, with considerable loss, by this synchronised dawn attack.

Cholera made its appearance in July at Wadi Halfa, and in an attempt to escape from the infection, the Regiment was marched twenty miles south to Gemai. There were eighteen deaths from cholera and nine from typhoid that month. The outbreak was not entirely surprising, as the Regiment had been drawing their water from the Nile at Wadi Halfa downstream of the native lines, although there was a filtering system.

Next, the north wind, which was depended upon to sail up the Nile, failed to blow for forty days. Furthermore, there was a succession of unprecedented rainstorms which washed away the railway line, further conspiring against Lord Kitchener and his forces. The Regiment welcomed rebuilding the railway line as a break from their monotony.

In early September, Lord Kitchener was ready to advance at last. On 11th September the Regiment embarked for Kosheh, and advanced in three steamers and some towed barges towards Dongola. Nearly 200 men had to be left behind when a fourth steamer broke down.

The Dervish Army was met 'dug in' by the Nile, at Hafir, on 19th September. The main force of Egyptians, along with the Staffords out of the barges, advanced on the Dervish position, whilst the three steamers with the rest of the Regiment sailed on to outflank the enemy's position. Though the steamers were hit by the Sudanese guns a number of times, they succeeded in passing the enemy positions and fired on them from the rear, whilst the outflanking Staffords enfiladed the enemy trenches with rifle and Maxim gun fire. This was too much for the Dervishes, who broke and fled. Dongola was occupied on 23rd September, and the brief campaign was over. The Regiment re-embarked for Cairo. Lord Kitchener complimented the Regiment for its efforts, and the Prince of Wales's (North Staffordshire) Regiment was later awarded the battle honour, HAFIR, carried by no other British regiment. Following a year in Cairo, the 1st Battalion went to India, and were stationed in the Punjab and then Jhansi in the United Provinces.

The Sudan medal group to Pte. W. Green.

In 1899 war broke out between Britain and the Boer republics of the Transvaal and the Orange Free State in South Africa. It was an inevitable conflict, fought to decide whether British or Boer would be supreme in southern Africa. The Prince of Wales's (North Staffordshire) Regiment was not involved in the initial stages of the conflict. The 1st Battalion was still in India, and the 2nd Battalion was in its peacetime station in Newry, Ireland. The 2nd Battalion were soon ordered to embark for Aldershot, in December 1899, to mobilise, and they would arrive in South Africa the following February.

They joined the 15th Brigade of the 7th Division of Lord Robert's main army, in preparation to cross the Modder River into the Free State. The 1st East Lancashires, 2nd South Wales Borderers and 2nd Cheshires were the other units of this Brigade. The 15th February saw the first engagement with the Boers at Jacobsdal, where a steady open order advance was made against their positions.

However, the Boers slipped away before the North Staffords could close. The engagement only cost the Regiment three men wounded. Remaining in Jacobsdal for three

A.303 Long Lee rifle, Standard British Army
issue throughout the Boer War.

weeks prevented the North Staffords taking part in the battle of Paardeberg and the surrender of the Boer General, Cronje; but they took an active part in the victorious advance on Bloemfontein, the Free State capital, and were numbered amongst the first troops to occupy it.

Boer commandos (units) were still close by, so after a week, the 7th Division moved out, and fought in the successful engagement at Karee Siding which eliminated the Boers' immediate threat. Lord Roberts now prepared for the 260 mile advance on Johannesburg, the centre of the goldfields, and Pretoria, the capital of the Transvaal, 40 miles further on. On 3rd May the North Staffords started northwards and entered Johannesburg on 31st May. Just before they had entered Johannesburg, a Volunteer Company, formed from the 1st and 2nd Volunteer Battalions, joined them.

A number of minor actions occurred but the Boers only offered a token resistance to the advance, which comprised of a series of long hot marches and many deployments. A destroyed railway bridge was one allotted task of the North Staffords, and then a four day march of 73 miles, taking only twenty-one and a half hours to cover the last 38 miles to Kroonstad. That earned the regiment a pat on the back from Lord Roberts. The Mounted Infantry Company saw more action and were probably envied by the bulk of the 2nd Battalion.

It was the destiny of the 15th Brigade to garrison Johannesburg for the next eight months, finding themselves on not unfamiliar police duties. Johannesburg was the main concentration of Uitlanders (non-Boers) in the Transvaal, and looting by Kaffir mine workers was a continual problem.

Boer commandos became more active at the latter stages of the North Staffords occupation of Johannesburg. In August and September the Regiment formed part of the columns despatched to engage Boer concentrations. The main engagement, in the Klip River vicinity, was when they encountered the hidden Boers in thick fog, and a nasty situation seemed likely. However the Boers evacuated as soon as the fog lifted.

Leaving Johannesburg in January 1901, the Regiment received high praise from the civil authorities. They joined the mobile column of Brigadier-General Dartnell, providing the marching element of his column, which was otherwise made up of mounted infantry and artillery. They were sweeping the area lying between the two railways running to Delagoa Bay and into Natal, in the Eastern Transvaal, along with another four separate columns. Their objective was not only to keep the Boers on the run, but also to apply a scorched earth policy by destroying crops and removing the inhabitants of farms. Although there were virtually no engagements, the troops were continually on the move for three months and had plenty of

A Victorian period Sergeant's band tunic and blue cloth helmet.

hardship to endure, often on short rations or living off the country. There was constant heavy rain and only bullock carts for transport.

In the meantime the Mounted Infantry Company operated in the West of the country, chasing the Boer guerrilla leader De La Rey, and were present at his defeat and capture at Wildfontein. Later they distinguished themselves by helping to beat off a determined Boer attack on a convoy at Platberg, whilst acting as part of the escort.

The close of April saw the North Staffords at the Wakkerstroom township near the Natal border, and 20miles away on the Volkrust railway in the Transvaal. The British decided to build lines of blockhouses to divide the country into sectors and impede the movement of the Boers, their supplies and munitions. This task of course fell onto the shoulders of the hard-worked infantry. The initial lines of blockhouses were along the railways and were completed by July 1901, when they started the cross-country lines of blockhouses. By October one such line from Derby (close to the border with Swaziland), the 43miles to Wakkerstroom, had been completed. By February 1902, the gap westwards to Volkrust was also complete.

Curved double sheets of corrugated iron filled with shingle formed the standard blockhouse walls. These were sited 1,000 yards apart and connected by barbed wire fences, with tin cans and the like hung on them to give away the presence of intruders. Seven men would be the normal garrison for each blockhouse.

In the Wakkerstroom area no large bodies of Boers were able to get through, though it was virtually impossible to stop the odd one crossing the lines. Lack of sleep for the men proved to be the biggest drawback of the blockhouses, over long periods of time. Blockhouses

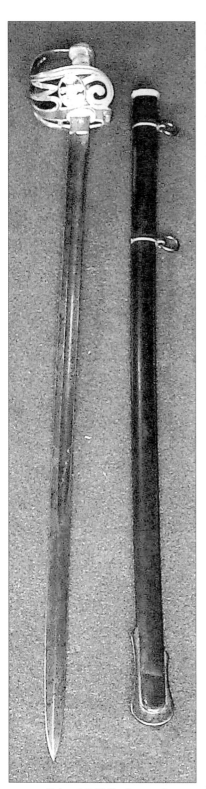

Colonel E.V. Fox's sword.

had not been intended to commit soldiers to purely static defence, rather a firm base from which mobile columns could operate. The Staffords Mounted Infantry took their full share in these operations.

Back in June 1900, the 4th Battalion the Prince of Wales's (North Staffordshire) Regiment went out to South Africa as well, receiving an additional 150 reinforcements from the 2nd Battalion. The 1st Battalion found a number of additional detachments to replace drafts it sent to the 2nd Battalion in South Africa. The 4th Battalion was deployed in the south west of the Cape Colony, as a number of Boer commandos units had escaped southwards and were trying to stir up the Boers in the Cape.

A far superior force of the enemy attacked a detachment of the 4th Battalion occupying the small town of Richmond, in June 1901. The main positions in the buildings held out all day though some small posts in sangars on kopjes overlooking the town were overrun. Fortunately for the defenders the Boers withdrew in the evening.

By 1902 the blockhouse policy had started to take effect, and peace was finally signed in the May. In March the men originally sent to the 4th Battalion from the 2nd Battalion rejoined the 4th, having been replaced by the 3rd Battalion, now in the Bechuanaland Protectorate manning a 37 mile blockhouse line. The 2nd Volunteer Company who had replaced the 1st in June 1901 returned home. In August the Mounted Infantry Company rejoined the North Staffords and they embarked finally in September, at Durban, for England. Though they had seen little hard fighting, they had done all that was asked of them during a hard two and a half years. The Regiment earned five DSOs and seven DCMs. The Prince of Wales's (North Staffordshire) Regiment was awarded the battle honour, SOUTH AFRICA 1900-1902.

On their arrival at Lichfield, at 2am, the North Staffords received a fantastic reception with the local Fire Brigade lighting their march through the city with torches. There was an equally good send off when the 2nd Battalion left again for India in 1903.

When the 2nd Battalion arrived at Bombay they met the 1st Battalion for the first time. The 2nd Battalion's initial station was in the Punjab at Amballa, then on to Dagshai in the hills. They had to move during the hot

A Boer War Tribute illuminated scroll to Lance Corporal A C Ward of the 2nd VB of the
North Staffordshire Regiment from Burton on Trent (who produced this type of scroll as
an alternative to a tribute medal).

weather, but soldiering conditions had nevertheless changed in India. Troops were no longer left for years, in hot stations on the plains, to sweat it out. A detachment would be left for internal security, whilst the rest of the regiments moved to a hot weather station for six months of a year. When stations were close, the men would march there, otherwise movement would be by troop train to the foothills and then a march.

Keeping the troops occupied was the usual problem, so sports were encouraged, with the North Staffords winning the Armyin India and Football cups, in 1904. Drink continued to cause trouble. The Royal Army Temperance Society's billiard and coffee rooms, and 'drink-free' medals for years 'on the wagon', were well supported by the authorities. Reproductions of the colours were very popular in needlework competitions.

Officers enjoyed plentiful leave, which they could afford to take, unlike the rank and file. Five officers are recorded as being on twelve months leave outside India, and three others on two or three months leave in India, whilst the rest of the regiment sweated in temperatures of 111° F. in 1907.

There was a lull before the 1914-1918 Great War storm, and it was a dull period for the regiment. The most interesting event was the four infantry and one cavalry divisions concentrated into Rawalpindi for the Prince of Wales's review by Lord Kitchener. 1909 saw the Regiment in Peshawar and aiding the civil authorities to deal with that turbulent city's communal disturbance in 1910.

On June 28th 1914, the Austrian Archduke Franz Ferdinand was assassinated by a Serb in Sarajevo. Just over a month later the major powers of Europe were at war. Britain entered the conflict on 4th August as a result of the German invasion of Belgium, and on 12th August, the British Expeditionary Force began landing in France. The plume and knot of the North Staffords was worn by eighteen battalions in all during the Great war, and 4,000 men would lose their lives serving with them.

Pte A. Rowbotham's Boer War Tribute Medal group.

Four original and contemporary South Stafford silk postcards

Ten
The History of The South Staffordshire Regiment during the Great War 1914-1918: From the Diary

Austrian Archduke Franz Ferdinand was assassinated in Sarajevo on June 28th 1914; a month later Europe was at war. Britain entered the conflict on 4th August with the German invasion of Belgium. Though 17 battalions ultimately wore the knot and crown and 5,999 soldiers died with the South Staffords, space limits an attempt to do them all justice, so I will concentrate on the 1st and 2nd Battalions.

The 2nd Battalion, at the time in Aldershot in the 6th Brigade, were the first South Staffs into action, after 5 days. They had a slow, uncomfortable train journey to Le Cateau where they alighted. After 5 days, firing from Mons was heard and trenches dug. But the 2nd Division eventually retreated, withdrawing under fire to Maroilles. The Germans advanced, hard fighting by the Guards only just allowing Maroilles to be evacuated, under fire.

A contemporary postcard of the South Staffords camp at Moore Park dated 1913.

The Staffords lost 17 men ("missing"), most taken prisoner as they slept. On 1st September the 6th Brigade passed through the Guards, taking over from the Guards as they withdrew, having suffered severely. A battery on the edge of a nearby wood was heavily shelled, 2 Stafford companies repelled the enemy; the A company under Capt. Savage, took over high ground to draw fire. Despite shelling and machine-gun fire, they did not engage the enemy. The guns were saved, and A and part of D companies withdrew carrying some wounded. One man was killed, 26 wounded, 34 missing. The retreat continued, and the furthermost point reached was Chaumes, 25 miles South East of Paris. The Battalion marched 236 miles in 16 days. On the 6th September, advancing towards the Marne, the Staffords saw many enemy dead and prisoners, showing the speed of the enemy's orderly retreat.

The 6th Brigade went into action at Hautevesnes, against a German rearguard, but under artillery fire, the enemy, whose guns had withdrawn, suffered heavy casualties. The two companies of Staffords in action had only slight loss. As the 5th Brigade crossed the Aisne, heavy fire could be heard. At Moussy, shells fired at a battery, hit some Staffords including Capt. Duckworth, who informed the King he had to be removed by lorry - thus immediately speeding up the provision of ambulances. An attack was launched where part of the Battalion supported the King's and was stopped by machine guns, causing both units to dig in. This heralded the beginning of trench warfare.

The 1st South Staffords were mobilised by 1st October 1914 as part of the 22nd Brigade, 7th Division, and embarked from Southampton for Belgium on 4th October, to reinforce the British Naval Brigade at Antwerp. They landed at Zeebrugge, and found that the Germans were between the 7th Div. and Antwerp. The 1st Battalion covered a canal crossing on the Ghent road, allowing the passage of the rearguard. Barricades and forward trenches were dug only for the bridge to be ordered to be blown up. When the loss of Antwerp was announced, the Division was pleased to find they had been of great assistance in its evacuation.

The retreat was resumed to Ypres where good food and good billets made a welcome change. The 22nd Brigade then held a position at Zonnebeke until they received orders to seize the Lys crossing at Menin.

The Staffords protected the left flank of the 21st Brigade attacking Klayhoek. The 1st Battalion came under heavy fire with little loss. Enemy forces trying to cut off the 7th Division, sparked another retreat. The 1st Battalion covered the withdrawal re-occupying the trenches at Zonnebeke, the Division holding part of the Ypres salient east of Gheluvelt with the enemy outnumbering them 5 to 1.

The 2nd Battalion used the same billets as the 1st Battalion. On the 23rd October, the 2nd Battalion recaptured trenches with bayonet charges, lost at Pilckem on the previous evening. Casualties included three officers - difficult to replace. The 2nd Battalion rejoined the 6th Brigade behind Zonnebeke, en route to the line north of the Salient, and relieved the Royal Berkshires after two days, advancing towards the woods of Passchendaele under heavy shell fire. On the edge of the forest 250 Germans pretended to surrender with white flags, then opened fire. After bloody retaliation the angry Staffords dug in, opposite the surviving treacherous enemy.

The 2nd Battalion advanced with the K.R.R. (Kings Royal Regiment) on their left, but both halted on reaching strongly fortified high ground south of Passchendaele. On the 29th, the 1st Division was fiercely assaulted, and simultaneously, enemy artillery pinned down the 2nd Division, who were then attacked next day after another bombardment. The enemy reached the wire, but despite desperate attacks, in the presence of the Kaiser, were beaten off with great loss. The 2nd Division trenches were then heavily shelled.

In an attack on Becelaere village, the Staffords were on the left. The morning mist stopped artillery support, the troops going forward as the mist cleared until the French were stopped by heavy fire. The 2nd Division had various detached units, no trained staff and confused orders. The 2nd Battalion and the Connaught Rangers repulsed the Germans, prior to heavy enemy artillery fire. Two determined attacks by Capt. Kilby's company forced the enemy out of some woods, as French reinforcements restored their line.

Many attacks were repulsed in the next nine days, and despite mounting casualties, the line held firm, even with the nearest German posts only 10 yards from the British trenches. The Germans sapped to within 45 yards of the Staffords, using what the War Diary describes as *"light Artillery very near their firing line"*, probably mortars. The French withdrew, but the Staffords isolated posts held out until the end. One platoon held a redoubt in a spinney until 18 were killed; one survivor, a sergeant, escaped wounded and was captured; the enemy were dead and lying thick around the bodies of this gallant little band. But the 2nd Battalion casualties were low compared with others.

The Prussian Guard made a viscious attack on the 12th November, and the French withdrew allowing Germans behind the 2nd Battalion, but though they were in extreme peril they were full of fight. With meagre reinforcements the dwindling 2nd Battalion eventually withdrew from their gallantly held trenches to the new French line. Next day the attack ceased. The first Battle of Ypres was over, and the German thrust had halted, but at an awful cost. The 2nd Division alone, had lost 227 officers and over 5,500 other ranks and the other British divisions much the same. On 16th November they were relieved, and they marched to Caestre for the first real rest since the war began.

On 20th October the 1st South Staffs on the Ypres Salient were assaulted by German infantry with artillery support. From the enemy line, 500 yards away, there were more attacks supported by shelling, just missing the Stafford trenches. The accurate sustained rifle fire caused heavy German losses - their survivors thought the fire was from machine guns, of which there were still only two per battalion. 4.00 pm saw the badly mauled Queens and Royal Welsh withdraw, exposing the Staffords left flank to German infiltration in the darkness. Enemy shells had killed or wounded Battalion HQ's occupants, and most of the rations, ammunition, clothing and animals were destroyed.

At 4.00 am on the 22nd October, a withdrawl was ordered to Veldhoek on the Menin-Ypres road. Most Staffords made it, but the remains of the transport were captured on the way, all but a few of the drivers and escort were killed or POWs. Without supplies the survivors were in a sorry state; and many had not slept for 3 days. The countryside at Veldhoek was enclosed. Sub units were put into the line as they arrived and where they were needed, resulting in intermingling of regiments and confusion. The 23rd October was quiet, with only one company in action, and next day the company reinforced the Northumberland Hussars in leading an attack on a farm. Its popular commander, Dunlop, was killed, but promptly avenged by his men. The two regular battalions met in the line, and the first issue of rum was received by the 7th Division.

The 25th October saw the 1st Battalion send 3 companies to Kruiseik, SE of Gheluvelt, on attachment to the 20th Brigade. The other company, Capt. Ransford's D, on its way up to the trenches, captured 19 prisoners and then an enemy patrol, and were fired on by friend and foe alike. Later Ransford, already twice wounded, went forward to make a reconnaissance never to be seen again. Reinforcing the Grenadier Guards, the Staffords were approached by a body of men saying *"Don't shoot, we are Scots Guards and South Staffords"*, but with them all wearing picklehaubs they were greeted with a hail of bullets that few escaped. At the end of the night, the remnants of D Company, the Grenadier and Scots Guards, were heavily shelled in the pouring rain. Suddenly the bombardment ceased and the obliterated trenches were full of Germans, and the only officer and few survivors of the company, were captured.

On the night of the 25/26th the surviving 3 companies were heavily shelled, and Ovens the Battalion C.O. made a new rear position with two platoons. Next morning a large body of troops were retiring. - Quartermaster White investigating was told they were ordered to withdraw. As this was a misunderstanding, he led the men under heavy fire to the rear, where Ovens redeployed them keeping the thinly held line intact.

After a lull, the enemy offensive of 29th hit the 7th Div. on either side of the Menin road to Ypres. Obscured by morning mist the overwhelming enemy forced the British back after the defenders had almost been annihilated. The 1st South Staffs and Royal Welch Fusiliers merged into one battalion under Ovens, holding the line until a new position was dug east of Gheluvelt. The Gordon Highlanders and a composite unit failed to retrieve the situation on the 30th and had heavy casualties.

The survivors of the 22nd Brigade dug in, and the fierce fighting on the 31st saw Ovens wounded and Major Loder-Symonds killed. Enemy attacks eased for 5 days but the shelling was relentless. On the 5th November the British front line re-adjusted, and on the 7th, the 22nd Brig. attacked an enemy trench north west of Klein Zillebeke, which the Staffords took and held with 3 enemy machine-guns. Aware of the Battalion's losses, Capt Vallentin in hospital at Ypres with a slight wound, rejoined his unit and though wounded again, led his men until he was killed. His gallant leadership resulted in the capture of the trench and was followed by a posthumous Victoria Cross. He was the first of the Bn. to receive the honour.

When Quartermaster White and the other surviving officers led the Staffords out of the trenches, only 78 of the 1,100 other ranks present at the start of the First Battle of Ypres were left. The 1st Bn. changed its 'Regimental Day' from 'Kirbekan' to 'Ypres' after the war.

A strong German attack captured most of Givenchy. British and French reinforcements rushed to the area, including the Staffords in the 2nd Division. Leaving Caestre in London buses on the 22nd, the Staffords relieved an Indian unit and a company of French infantry, holding a 1000 yard line between the La Bassee Canal and Givenchy. The enemy trenches were between 150-600 yards away. There was little shelling but the sniping was incessant.

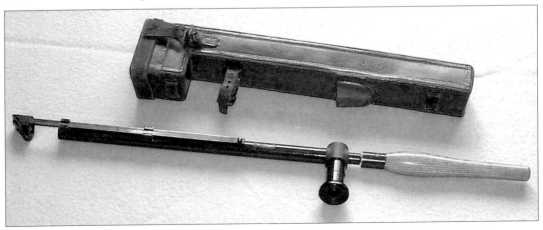

A contemporary officer's trench periscope

Although again in trenches half filled with water and surrounded by a vast sea of mud, the health of the troops was good apart from a little trench foot and frost bite. The Battalion moved to billets north of Bethune on the 26th, and saw in the new year there.

The 2nd Battalion spent 1915 in this small area suffering from the appalling weather. An issue of a few telescopic sights improved the sniping - the only form of aggression available.

Two companies of Glasgow Highlanders, and a Territorial battalion of the Highland Light Infantry were attached to the Staffords. The new horror of mining fuelled a big raid on the 20th to determine if a particular enemy trench was being used to sink a mine. No secret was made of the raid with a heavy bombardment and covering fire. No sign was found, but it was an extremely costly affair. A complete Territorial battalion, the 5th King's Liverpool Regiment, was then posted to the Brigade, with its companies attached to regular units for instruction.

The few 1st Battalion survivors received complimentary letters but few awards due to the lack of recommending officers at its rest camp near Bailleul. On 11th November 1914 they became Corps Troops to the 4th Corps at Merville. On the 13th December, after poor billets, they went back into the trenches with the 22nd Brigade. Some officers and men from other regiments rejoined from hospital, but they were still under strength. In support of the Queens and Royal Warwicks, and actually supporting the Warwicks right wing on the 18th December, the two assaulting Bn's were unable to hold the enemy trenches, the 1st Battalion evacuating the wounded. From the 20th, a quiet 5 days were spent before going back into reserve, and receiving a 500 man draft, 100 of whom were attached to the Queen's. The 1st Battalion finished 1914 in the trenches. Sniping caused several casualties, and rain caused floods. Enemy trenches and dug-outs were more ingenious in their construction and with better man management held with less men in more comfort.

The 1st Battalion moved to Laventie, east of Merville, taking over trenches on the 5th March. The 1st Battalion attacked the Pierre Redoubt on 12th March after 2 days in reserve. Mist prevented artillery support and there was little progress. Attached to the 21st Brigade, the Battalion attempted on two consecutive days to get to the trenches splashing around in the mud and stumbling into water filled shell holes, the guides getting lost on both occasions and the Battalion suffering a number of casualties.

The 2nd Division near Givenchy made a diversionary attack to confuse the enemy in the use of his reinforcements. At 7.30am on 10th March, the apparently unsurvivable British Bombardment started, with the 2nd Battalion column to the right, K.R.R. to the left and Liverpools in the centre. B company of the Battalion suffered heavy, accurate machine gun fire on leaving its trench. Fifteen men and a subaltern ordered to silence one of these guns did not return. Some troops made the enemy lines to be bombed out, and the survivors withdrew. A second bombardment failed to cut the enemy wire, or damage the trenches and machine gun emplacements.

In the afternoon attack C company had even less to show for their losses, and the attack was called off. Though the troops had tried their best, the staff work was faulty and the afternoon's attack should have been abandoned. The Battalion lost seven officers and about 130 other ranks. The gains were less than expected, but straightened the British line and allowed better observation. The 2nd Division's costly attack prevented enemy reinforcements reaching Neuve Chapelle.

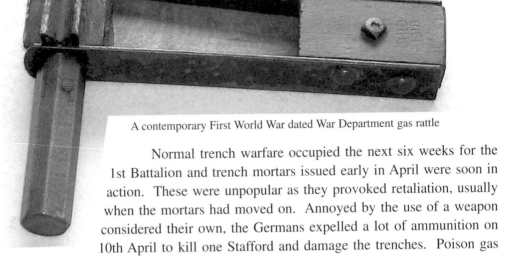

A contemporary First World War dated War Department gas rattle

Normal trench warfare occupied the next six weeks for the 1st Battalion and trench mortars issued early in April were soon in action. These were unpopular as they provoked retaliation, usually when the mortars had moved on. Annoyed by the use of a weapon considered their own, the Germans expelled a lot of ammunition on 10th April to kill one Stafford and damage the trenches. Poison gas also saw its debut this month in the second battle of Ypres.

After a series of moves, on 10th May the 1st Battalion were near Bethune, and the 2nd Battalion also spent the next 6 weeks training or in the trenches. A new enemy surprise appeared in the form of the 'whiz-bang', a new small shell that unlike the heavier shells and mortar bombs burst before it could be heard or seen. The Germans viciously shelled the 1st Battalion on 22nd April but with light casualties.

On 8th May, the 2nd Division was briefed to attack Festubert one mile north of Givenchy, but the bombardment had been inadequate, and unbroken enemy wire brought the infantry to a stop. The 1st Battalion supported the 6th Brigade attack on the night of the 15th, D Company reinforced the K.R.R occupying the enemy trenches, and the remainder were in close support. Severe casualties were sustained from heavy shelling, and the next day seven officers were hit. Two of C company's platoons carried stores forward despite mounting losses from enemy fire.

The 1st Battalion relieved the K.R.R early on the 17th May, and attacked the Cour d'Avouene Farm from the north at 10.30am, the 5th Brigade to their left, the Liverpools on the right. The right Battalion of the 5th Brigade were held up while assaulting another farm, and the Staffords suffering a deadly enfilade fire. A D company platoon had pushed on towards a dyke north of the objective, and were trying to reinforce it. Lt. Col Routledge was killed, and three other officers wounded. Cour d'Avouene still held out. There was a further attack in the afternoon, when B supporting C, were pinned down, holding on grimly with mounting losses for 8 hours. The Battalion finally handed over to the Liverpool Territorials the next day.

Of one thousand who went into battle 3 days previously, 130 marched back to Bethune, though some rejoined the next day and the reserve brought the strength up to 418. Two officers and 41 other ranks were dead, 9 officers and 404 other ranks wounded and 75 missing, many of whom were dead.

The 1st Battalion, in action 2 miles South, had faired rather better. The 22nd Brigade attacked at 3.15am on 16th May, the Royal Welch Fusiliers to the left, the Queens on the right, supported by Warwicks and the 1st Battalion. A preliminary assault on the left was hoped to distract the enemy, improving the surprise, whilst a bombardment of several days was designed to soften the defences and conceal the time of the attack.

Going forward, the Queens, 150 yards in front of the Staffords, who now occupied their trenches, were mown down by enemy gun-fire. A renewed British barrage, following a pause, caused havoc in the enemy lines making the second advance far more successful. Advancing by companies, the 1st Battalion entered the enemy trenches to the right of the Queens and bombed out the occupants, and due to Capt Bonner's leadership, and Lt Hassell's bombers, the objective was consolidated.

Heavy German shelling rained down from dawn on the 17th, reaching its climax on the afternoon of the 18th. But as the enemy losses had been severe no infantry counter-attack materialised, and despite the heavy shelling the trenches were repaired. At midnight, on 18/19th May, the unit was relieved, and the weary survivors were billeted in Bethune, having lost 270 casualties of whom only two were missing. The marshy ground fortunately caused the harmless explosion of many enemy shells.

Some lessons from Neuve Chapelle had been learned, but communication between gunners and infantry was still faulty, and the enemy losses, and the small gain, hardly justified the grievous casualties and shell expenditure.

After Festubert, the 2nd Battalion, after reinforcements, was in the line east of Bethune, at Cambrin, and had an exciting experience. On 29th June a trap was set for the enemy with the explosion of a small mine, followed by another. Expecting an attack the Germans rushed up reserves, and were greeted by an artillery barrage and rapid fire from the Staffords, cheering loudly as if about to attack. When it was thought the enemy trenches were fully manned, a third - and very big - mine was set off, with disastrous results to the Germans. The enemy shelling, prior to the mines, varied; one officer and seven men had been killed and ten wounded from a vicious barrage. In the retaliation for the mines, one man was wounded. Prolonged rain in August and September half flooded 2nd Battalion trenches, making preparations for the coming offensive more difficult.

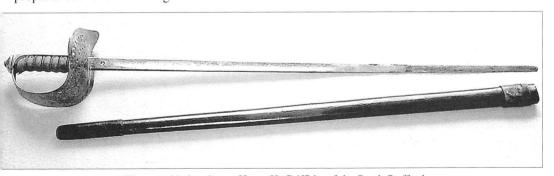

The sword belonging to Henry H. Griffiths of the South Staffords

The 1st Battalion had a quiet time between Festubert and Loos, with Ovens resuming command of the 1st Battalion The 7th Division left the Ypres Salient to an area south of the La Bassee Canal covering Vermelles. Hitherto occupied by the French, they and the Germans were keeping themselves well apart. This new front was narrow and there was now a lot of new trench digging in No Man's Land indicating a new offensive.

The plan was for the British to attack, with the 1st and 4th Corps, south of the La Bassee Canal to the Bethune-Lens road, the 5th Corps making a secondary or holding attack east of Ypres. The main objectives of the southern attacks were the Hohenzollern Redoubt, Fosse 8, the Quarries, Cite St. Elie, the village of Wingles Meurchin across the canal from Lille to Douai. The mining village of Loos, from which the battle got its name, was about 2 miles north west of Lens, to the south of the 6 mile sector. The 2nd Division was concerned with the northern area, each side of the La Bassee Canal, which now consisted of the 5th, 6th and 19th Brigades. The 6th Brigade still had five battalions, but the Hertfords had replaced the Territorial unit of the King's Liverpools.

Both front lines in the 6th Brigade sector were in an extensive brickfield, with stacks of bricks in and behind the forward trenches about 200 yards apart. The connecting ground was pitted with mine craters, some of which were used by the Germans in his defences, connected to their trenches, so that in some places the opposing troops were only 25 yards apart. These craters funnelled the British into narrow lines of advance through enemy machine guns. A four day bombardment of the enemy lines was to precede the attack, and the allies would use poison gas for the first time. The 2nd South Staffords were to the left of the 6th Brigade, the 1st King's on the right, supported by the Royal Berkshires and the Hertfords, the K.R.R. in reserve. The part of the enemy line allocated to the Staffords was as strong as any on the front - there was no flank approach possible. C Company, to the left, were to advance up the towpath and assault the Embankment Redoubt strong-point. A and B to the right, had the objectives of some brick-stacks, for fear of damage to their gas cylinders.

Unfortunately the wind was unfavourable, the Royal Engineers officer-in-charge gas refused to take responsibility. Despite this, an officer from Corps or Division ordered the gas switched on, with appalling results. It should have been obvious that a senior officer was needed on the spot to make such a decision. The gas poured back into the British lines and the attack was doomed before it began. The Germans even lit bonfires on their parapets to turn back the gas, so the enemy knew its use was contemplated.

There was no hope of surprise. It was further given away by the 5th Brigade attacking 30 minutes before the rest of the Division. Once the unfortunate troops, denied any chance of success, attacked at 6.30, half choked and blinded by gas, they were at once victim to rifle fire, and fire from well-concealed machine guns. C Company, under Capt. Kilby, gallantly advanced up the towpath, despite many men suffering from gassing. Murderous fire met this company from both sides of the canal, as the 5th Brigade had been unable to advance. Wounded as soon as he left the trench, Kilby continued to lead his men to the enemy wire and into a shower of grenades as well as point-blank small arms fire. He was shot down and also lost a foot, but despite this continued to use a rifle and cheer on his men until he was killed. His posthumous VC was well-earned. His company was closely supported by 2nd Lieut. Williams machine gun, who kept his gun firing until all but one of its crew were dead, despite being wounded.

Meanwhile, to the right, A and B were pinned down a few yards from their starting line, Boyd-Moss reporting to Brigade, to advance or continue the attack would be suicidal, and consequently he was ordered to withdraw to allow the heavy artillery to shell the enemy positions. However this fire was inaccurate falling on the enemies rear trenches and ruling

Webly VI revolver, the standard revolver of British Officers in the First World War

out any possibility of success. The Battalion was relieved by the Berkshires about midday, though some volunteers waited until dark then brought in the wounded, some from only a few yards from the enemy wire. The Berkshires were hurriedly moved and the 2nd South Staffords were back in line by 2.00 am.

Another attempt to support the 1st Corps was abandoned, after patrols were heavily fired upon. Heavy rain over the next few days slowed up the battle, and the Battalion was properly relieved on 30th September, having lost, in addition to the ten officers, 129 other ranks killed, missing or wounded, and 130 cases of gas poisoning. All the 2nd Division had managed to do in this disastrous battle, was tie down German troops from going where the British attacks were more successful.

The 7th Division, to the right of the 2nd Division, contained the 22nd Brigade at the left of the Division front. The Warwicks were on the left, the 1st South Staffs on the right, the Royal Welch Fusiliers in support and the Queens in reserve. In front lay deep, well wired trenches; behind these a group of quarries, and to the left, the Hohenzollern Redoubt, linked to a coal mine with a high slag heap, Fosse 8. The attack was north east, and the enemy defences with well-sited machine guns almost impervious to shell fire, were indeed formidable.

During the 24th September, the 1st Battalion awaited the assault in acute discomfort in flooded trenches, moving forward at night through a maze of muddy ditches to its start off position. C Company was in the front line, A and D in support trenches approximately 80 yards behind with B close behind D. A gas and smoke barrrage was the prelude to the attack. The gas caused a few casualties amongst the Battalion, but the smoke, helped by drizzle and mist, concealed C, who went "over the top" at 6.30am. Though losing three company commanders, the advance, in extended order, made steady progress, despite much uncut wire, and the forward German lines were stormed. The Quarries were also taken and a group under Ovens almost reached the La Bassee-Lens road, taking 200 prisoners, but by this time attacking units were well mixed up.

Strong defences in front, and increasing casualties, caused Ovens to retire to the partially consolidated Quarries, but with the enemy having infiltrated back, as the Staffords beat off a frontal attack, they and the Green Howards found themselves with the Germans behind them too. Young, the C.O. of the Green Howards, and Ovens were well ahead with a small mixed company, and they were under an accurate fire from the British artillery who thought the enemy had retaken the quarries, through which Ovens and Young had to return to the old enemy line. Back at the old enemy line heavy shelling and bombing caused severe loss. Both C.O.s went back to the quarries with the men they could raise, only to find them full of the enemy, and they had to fight their way back. At this point, General Capper, the 7th Division Commander, was fatally wounded.

The decimated 22nd Brigade held these former enemy trenches from 27th-30th September, against repeated attacks and despite continual artillery fire, fighting from muddy trenches in pouring rain against greatly superior forces. The Battalion machine gunners and bombers were of great service. The Brigade was relieved on the 30th, but after only two nights was ordered south of the canal. Fortunately for the depleted and exhausted Division, this was a quiet sector, apart from shellfire. On the 13th, the last effort at a gas attack was ineffective and no assault was tried, though there was still hostile retaliation.

Little had been achieved, and modest captures of ground were far outweighed by an enormous casualty list, the 1st Battalion losing well over half its strength. One of the few surviving officers was Ovens, the only C.O. left in the Brigade. The biggest lesson from Loos was that German grenades were still far superior; a reliable and effective bomb was urgent and the need was not fully met by the Mills.

Following Loos, Boyd-Moss started special training for the bombers of the 2nd Battalion and tried methods to seal off portions of trenches; both these being adopted by the 6th Brigade. On 13th October a new weapon, eleven-inch mortar bombs, fell on the units billets, causing severe damage and fifteen casualties. At this time both the trenches and billets were bad, causing a good deal of sickness. The Kings reported that there was a white cross on their front, erected by the Germans, and inscribed: *"For King and Fatherland. In memory of Lieutenant King and Lieutenant Hall and eight men of the South Staffordshire Regiment who died like heroes. Erected by O.S.P.A.R"* Even in this war their was some chivalry.

Two units from each Division were selected to attend an inspection by King George V on 28th October. It was indeed a high honour that these came from both batalions of the South Staffordshire Regiment. The majority of the officers present were young subalterns of whom few would survive the war.

The rain continued and sickness increased, but the Germans confined themselves to shelling which was largely ineffective, because of the thick mud, their infantry probably being in much the same state as our own. On 23rd November morale and march discipline had improved a little, with the 2nd Battalion forming a small corps of drums. This day saw the Battalion take over trenches in the Cambrin sector, south of La Bassee Canal, and having to also consolidate a large crater. It was unnerving work as it was believed that the Germans had been mining the crater. This was confirmed at 4.30pm on the 24th when a huge explosion buried and killed the working party of two officers and 24 men. A party under 2nd Lieut Carter, later C.O. of the 7th Battalion, re-occupied the crater and vigorously replied to the shower of bombs and rifle grenades, but the three officers present were wounded and there was a temporary evacuation. Another party at once occupied the crater, holding it until relieved. Besides the first party killed by the mine, there were three wounded officers, a further 10 men killed and 33 wounded. It was a bad day for the unit.

A contemporary postcard of the South Staffords

The year ended with more rain and snow making supplying the front dangerous and tiring - the enemy gunners had a thorough knowledge of the ground and their fire was effective. Meanwhile some of the drafts now contained men over 40, the war diary points out these were rarely able to deal with the rigors of trench life in winter; so still the unit was well under establishment. During 1916 there was an increase in comfort and cleanliness in billets, and they were fairly free of enemy shelling. Becoming part of the 4th Corps, in March, the 2nd Division moved to a sector south of Loos, and here the billets in cellars were superior - some even had beds! Walshe took over from Morgan only to be reposted a few days later. Much damage and loss was caused by enemy mortars and rifle grenades, and when the Battalion was next out of the line, the bombing section made a detailed study of the layout and ranges of the enemy trenches from maps and ariel photographs. When the unit went back, the bombers, under an energetic subaltern, went into action with great enthusiasm. If the enemy fired a grenade they immediately got two or more back and thus they lost the initiative.

Much emphasis was laid on raiding, and replica trenches made of those it was proposed to visit. But an elaborate raid on 14th May failed. The two parties involved came back prematurely thinking whistles, blown by the Germans, were recall signals. This lesson had not been learnt later that month when the unit had moved to Vimy Ridge, and were ordered to reconnoitre a captured British trench. Four parties were used this time, preceeded by an ineffective mortar bombardment, that failed to cut the enemy wire and alerted the Germans. Two parties failed to reach the enemy wire and the two that did were forced to retire without any information. Confusing signals and lack of control hindered the raid, that had no chance of sucess anyway, after the futile mortar fire. Three officers and seven other ranks were lost, in what the regimental history describes as a gallant attempt; all taking part being volunteers. However the bombing section, backed up by the mortars, now replied to the German rifle grenades so quickly, and accurately, that after 2 days the enemy refused to provoke them.

The 1st Battalion were near Bethune in billets or in the trenches south of La Bassee Canal, about 6 weeks after Loos. The 7th Division then moved to rest camps near Amien, having a real break from the trenchs at last. The B.E.F reorganisation near the end of 1915 saw the Queens and South Staffs from the 22nd Brigade go to the 91st. The Territorial units of the 7th Division Brigades reverted to four units, the 91st consisting of the 2nd Queens, the 1st South Staffs, and the 21st and 22nd Manchesters.

The 7th Division then moved north of the Somme in February 1916, and though the Battalion's snipers dealt with those opposite, there was no British reply to the active enemy artillery due to the British shortage of ammunition. The trenches here were in a shocking state, even without enemy interference, the men having all they could manage to do to keep the slimy ditches barely habitable. Out of the line at Bray-sur-Somme there was occasional football matches, one played under shell and mortar fire that was ignored by players and spectators alike. The enemy gun-fire increased without effective response, and casualties were consistent and heavy. On the 20th May, four officers, the RSM, a CSM and 2 NCOs were hit, and on the 31st, more than 700 shells fell in the Battalion's sector, killing or wounding 20 other ranks. A high spot in this gloom was when Lewis gunners caught an enemy working party in the open, and on the 31st when our guns suddenly and effectively replied to the German bombardment. June was spent working in the trenches or in preparation for the looming Somme offensive.

Here the enemy front was about twelve miles astride the River Ancre, two miles from its northern boundary. It continued south to Fricourt, east of Albert, turning east for a mile or so and then south again towards the Somme. The German lines overlooked the British as far south as Montauban, where the ground was nearly level. Along this front the enemy, who had held it for nearly two years, had made extremely strong lines of trenches, with deep concreted bomb-proof shelters, lavishly protected by broad belts of wire entanglements secured to iron stakes. Their wire was of four belts, and so thick and resilient that even when cut by gunfire it still formed an impassable obstacle.

With the greatest preliminary bombardment ever the British hoped that powerful infantry attacks would pierce the enemy lines, denying the Germans of their observation posts so that open warfare could develop. On 24th June the artillery began firing over a million shells between then and 1st July. The divisional objective was the enemy trenches in front of Mametz, to the south of the front, north of the Montauban Ridge, the village itself and the second line behind. The 22nd Brigade was to the left and the 91st to the right, the Staffords on the left and the 22nd Manchesters were the other forward unit. Both Bn's were to have reserves for the capture of Mametz, and at zero plus 2 the Queens were to go through to the final objective. Special assembly trenches were dug behind the 7th Division front line, and though increasing the distance, saved many lives when the empty forward trenches were obliterated by an intense enemy bombardment just before the attack.

At 7.30am, on 1st July, the British barrage lifted, the leading waves advanced in square formation, and the first objective was overrun with slight cost. Fifteen minutes later the South Staffs were closing on Mametz, having covered 1,200 yards in 30 minutes - that was good going. D company, to the south, were held up, until reinforced by a company of 21st Manchesters, in close support. Most of Mametz was occupied after the many cellars and strong points were cleared by the bombers, and even some of the trenches beyond north east Mametz, but the final objective, a trench known as Bunny Alley, was still held by the enemy until 1pm, when a gallant company assault, led by Captain de Trafford took, but could not hold it. The village had been strongly garrisoned and many prisoners were taken from the dug outs dazed and demoralized by the terrific shelling that they declared was not war, but murder!

The forward Stafford companies in Bunny Alley withdrew into Mametz and consolidated and meanwhile the reserve battalion, the Queen's, had been committed. About 5pm, Morris arrived in Mametz with a mixed force of Staffords, Manchesters, Warwicks and Gordon Highlanders from the other Brigade, and went briskly into the attack, helped by supporting fire from the Queens, and taking the final objective at 8pm. Besides over 300 prisoners and machine guns, and stores, including engineer dumps, were captured, greatly assisting in the consolidation. Casualties were heavy, the South Staffs lost 10 officers and 350 other ranks, many from the confused fighting in Mametz. There was no German counter attack or shelling that night as the enemy gunners did not know the position of friend and foe, but next day 15 South Staffs were hit. The success of 1st July, for which the Battalion received congratulations for the part it had played, enabled the village of Fricourt to be pinched out the next day, and on the arrival of a fresh division, the advance continued.

On the 14th July, the 1st South Staffs dug in under heavy shell fire, in a valley behind the

A camouflaged British Brodie steel helmet

British front line, and in the afternoon the 91st Brigade were ordered to attack High Wood, moving to the assembly area through persistent shelling led by two companies of the Battalion on the left with the Queens on their right. One mile over the fields, lay the wood, as yet undamaged, but at the outset forward Germans were found in the hollows and shell holes, and killed or captured. On the right, rode detachments of British and Indian cavalry, until they were forced to dismount by machine gun fire. At about the same time, two of our planes swooped down to strafe the enemy with an interesting combination of modern and ancient warfare. Accurate machine gun fire from the left slowed down the Battalion, causing some loss, but the units forced their way into the forest, the dark adding to the difficulties. The Queens had captured the eastern edge of the wood by midnight and dug in; the Staffords were held up by a strong redoubt in the north west corner and gallant assaults by two platoons could not dislodge the enemy. The morning of the 15th saw fierce counter attacks forcing the Staffords back, so by dawn the northern and western parts of the wood were held by the enemy. A determined effort by the two Manchester battalions failed, on being held up by hidden machine guns.

The salient ahead of the British line, was becoming ever more difficult to sustain, its communications over open fields destroyed by German shelling. However rations and water were got through, though the evacuation of the wounded under fire from three sides was impossible by day and dangerous at night. It was decided to withdraw, these orders arriving only 90 minutes before these forward units were due out. This was largely accomplished by Ovens, the senior officer present. Dawn on the 18th saw the 91st Brigade retired with all the wounded who could be got away. All the gallantry and sacrifice were not altogether in vain, as the former German trenches in the rear had been adapted for British use.

The 1st Battalion could claim to have penetrated the German line, but it had suffered severely, the missing being very numerous owing to the confusion of units being mixed up and the dead and wounded lying hidden in the dense wood. Some of the 140 listed re-joined later, and some wounded were evacuated by other regiments. The 7th Division was again moved back to Amiens to reinforce and re-equip.

After 3 weeks sustained heavy fighting the German lines had been bent back north of the Somme, but there was no breakthrough, the enemy holding many strong points on the flanks and in front of the British. Amongst these were the Delville Wood's well fortified defences, 1,500 yards north west of Guillemont. Though not taking part in the first assaults on the wood, the 2nd Division moved up to this area on 25th July, taking over the former enemy support line near Montauban. The 2nd South Staffs and 17th Middlesex went forward in support of the 99th Brigade, now also in the 2nd Division, relieving a unit of Royal Fusiliers under constant shell fire to the north west front of the Wood. They were in touch with the 5th Division to the left and the intermingled Middlesex and K.R.R. on the right. The front followed the shape of the wood, the Staffs had C Company as a defensive flank facing west; A held the north edge, B was in support, and D in reserve. The Battalion had the most advanced position and were in extreme danger.

As the 99th Brigade withdrew, the German bombardment resumed with full fury, and 'B' Company's trenches were obliterated, its officers killed and most of the men buried. The survivors however, drove off German bombers approaching the wood. The other companies suffered in turn as their trenches were enfiladed by a heavy battery near Ginchy, being shelled from their front and flanks. Thus they were cut off, re-supply extremely dangerous by night and impossible by day, but an S.O.S. to the Division's artillery got through and as a result the enemy gunfire subsided.

On their relief on the night of 29th July, half of the Staffords were casualties, the three company commanders dead. There was further loss during the next two days in close support or at Carnoy. A large draft including men from Gallipoli had no steel helmets. Enemy air observation was active and preceded shelling, but did not stop a pleasant fraternisation when the 8th South Staffs moved into nearby billets. On the 4th August, the 8th South Staffs took over, and started improving the trenches and going forward to Trones Wood to treat the corpses with quicklime.

Following a brief respite, the 6th Brigade were in the attack, by the 2nd and 55th Divisions, on targets already attempted. 500 yards south of Delville Wood, in British hands, was Waterlot Farm and 1,200 yards south east of this was Guillemont village; both held by the enemy in strength and well fortified. The 6th Brigade was to capture the farm, the 17th Middlesex and 1st King's were to lead, the 2nd South Staffs in support and the 13th Essex in reserve. The attack was to be supported by an intense artillery bombardment; but there were disappointing results.

In summary and in brief, A Company was under the command of the King's, and B at the disposal of the Middlesex, under "Cabby" Carter, a gallant ranker officer, formerly a South Stafford. D was to support A if required and C was in reserve. The attack started at 4.30am, on the 8th August, but due to thick mist accounts of the early stages are confused. The three forward companies of the King's, on reaching their objective, were not seen again, being overwhelmed by a counter attack. At 5.30am A Company joined the remnants of the King's between Trones Wood and Guillemont, two platoons sent to hold and consolidate 'New' Trench. Meanwhile after taking their first objective, the Middlesex were held up by machine gun fire and intense bombing, so Carter called up the Staffords. Two and a half companies advanced to strengthen a rear position, because by the time they arrived the Middlesex forward companies had been overrun or forced back. The attack was postponed until the next day, and two units of the 5th Brigade took over part of the front.

At 2.30am on the 9th August, Carter's detachment assisted the assault on Machine Gun House, between Waterlot Farm and Guillemont, and the trench behind. A party of Staffords reached the trench on two occasions but were forced out by strong counter attacks. Artillery was requested and while it was being laid on, the Staffords supported an attack by the Essex. Before another assault could be made, the enemy guns assisted ours in shelling the enemy defenders, and whilst in progress the attack was called off, because with the continuing flow of enemy reinforcements there was no hope of success.

The Battalion was relieved that night to the billets with only slight loss. Visits were exchanged with the 1st Battalion. The 2nd had a change of C.O.s in August when Morgan was promoted to a Brigade and Dawes, another regular South Stafford, took over. On the 19th, the 2nd Div was posted to the 5th Corps moving to the Serre sector 8 miles north of Albert. In the War Diary of the 2nd Battalion for the 21st/22nd August: *"Two all quiet days of trenches. Front line blown in by minenwerfer and several casualties due to desultory field gun shelling"*. I suppose after the Somme this front did indeed seem quiet.

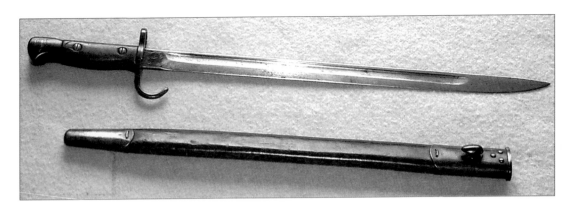

A 3rd Battalion South Staffs "Hooked Quillon" bayonet

The 7th Division were again in action in vile weather at the end of the month as the 1st South Staffs in Delville Wood. The front was of shell holes, waist deep in muddy water, linked with ditches that gave little protection. The Wood, following the prolonged fighting, was a sea of liquid mud, thickly covered in bodies that stank abominably, and behind the line conditions were so bad it took 4 hours to bring rations only 240 yards. Non stop bombardment on the 30th August and the morning of the 31st, preceded an enemy attack, led by lightly equipped bombers closely supported by masses of infantry. Both were hotly engaged by the Staffords and as the enemy withdrew their barrage again crashed down. When this lifted a second attack was again beaten off, but the situation was deteriorating for the diminishing Staffords. Bombs were low and the Lewis guns were all out of action, except one borrowed from the 1st North Staffs on the left, and no fresh supplies could be brought up through the barrage.

Undeterred by appalling losses, the brave and tenacious Germans put in a third attack, after another bombardment on the South Staffs, who, now without grenades and short of ammunition, fought grimly in the hand to hand struggle following. Courage was not enough to repel an enemy with endless reinforcements, well supplied with bombs and fresh into action against exhausted men, husbanding their last few bullets. Around 4.30pm, after aerial reconnaissance, the enemy artillery concentrated their fire, destroying the solitary supporting mortar; communication to our own guns was long since cut. At 8pm the final German attack forced the 30 forward company survivors back into Delville Wood where they held their ground reinforced by a trickle of other survivors. These sniped the enemy with their remaining ammunition until it got too dark and they received a welcome reinforcement by the Queens around midnight.

Meanwhile a third company fell back into the North Staffs trenches building a barricade that both Staffs Regiments defended stoutly until the Germans surprisingly and suddenly withdrew. On 1st September the 1st Battalion were relieved but remained in close support. In these three days, the 1st South Staffs lost a third of its strength, and few of the 146 missing were ever heard of again. The 400 men raised for a working party in the unsuccessful attacks on Ginch, were all that was available. Following a week in support there was a move to a rest area and Ovens left to command a Brigade, the last original Battalion commander and a most gallant and inspiring C.O. By now the Battalion was incapable of further action until rested, reinforced and re-equipped, when it was transferred to the 2nd Army on 18th September.

On 7th November the 2nd Battalion moved to Mailly in preparation for the forthcoming battle of Ancre, and to forming up trenches south of Serre. From here patrols checked the formidable German wire, and exploded a Bangalore torpedo under it. There was some surprise for there had been little shelling during the concentration on the night of the 12th. Four Divisions were to attack with powerful artillery support. The 3rd Division were on the left, the 2nd Division, left centre, its 6th and 5th Brigades, left and right. The Staffords were next to the 3rd Division, the Essex the other forward unit. The Battalion was of four waves with four platoons in the 1st, and two in the others, and close behind there were mopping up units to deal with the Germans, emerging from their deep dug outs, behind the first wave. Lewis guns were with these parties and four Vickers guns were on the flanks in support.

The attack started at 5.45am, on the foggy morning of the 13th November, preceded by a barrage. The Staffords, led by officers using compasses, slowly reached their first objective over the churned up ground. A few casualties were sustained by the left half company being too eager and being caught in their own barrage, but it otherwise went smoothly until the first wave got to the almost uncut wire protecting the enemy second line. There was a sudden rush of troops from the left from the 8th Brigade of the 3rd Division, who were not as well led as the 6th Brigade and had lost their way. In the confusion, the British barrage crept forward, and as it passed, the enemy machine gunners emerged from their dug outs, opening a murderous fire on the units struggling in the mud, in some places waist deep.

With rifles and Lewis guns jammed by the mud and grenades exhausted the South Staffs withdrew, taking their wounded with great difficulty with them and leaving their dead. A Stafford subaltern, who reached the enemy second line before being wounded, reported the Essex right company had carried its objective. Amongst the six officers of the Battalion killed were two company commanders, and all four CSMs were wounded; the amount of other casualties is unknown but must have been considerable.

The remnants of the brigade were formed into two composite battalions each under 300 strong, holding the line under prolonged shelling for two days. The enemy declined to attack in view of the state of No Man's Land. The Battalion was relieved on the 15th November and the following day the Division went to a rest area, leaving behind its artillery, as was often the case; it too had suffered severely.

This rest for the 7th Division, in September 1916, was a move north from the Somme to Bailleul, near the Belgian frontier, taking a section of trenches north of the river Lys. Relieving the Queens on the 27th, the 1st South Staffs found a front that had been static since created, the two systems of trenches between 500 to 1000 yards apart. Previous occupants of both sides having been content to improve their positions, leaving the enemy alone.

Though this peaceful mode was agreeable to the newly arrived, it did not suit the generals, who did not of course, live in the trenches. It was at once decided the enemy must be harassed and raided, three raids of which, by the Staffords, brought back prisoners and useful information. Such unmannerly antics were virtually ignored by the Germans. On the 3rd November, the 7th Div. was relieved, concentrated at St. Omer and then marched south east through rain, snow and fog reaching the line in front of the ruins of Beaumont Hamel north of Ancre by the 24th. These trenches were by now slimy holes in a vast area of thick, gluey mud, which had to be dug out at night. The enemy were close by and were alert and pugnacious, their snipers being particularly dangerous.

Out of the line, apart from enemy activity, conditions were little better. Mailly and Bertrancourt rest camps were flooded, muddy and depressing. Sniping and sickness took their toll, though the men bore their privations well. The sniping was not one sided; on one day the 91st Brigade claimed 15 victims. The only consolation was that, according to prisoners, conditions were almost equally as bad in the enemy trenches.

The 7th Div.'s positions were overlooked by the Germans. They made strenuous efforts to improve these and after minor sucesses by the 20th and 22nd Brigades, it was the turn of the 91st. Its objective was Munich Trench on a flat topped ridge 1 mile east of Beaumont Hamel. At dawn on 11th January 1917, the Brigade advanced with 3 battalions forward, the Staffords in the centre in thick fog under a sweeping barrage, which was stated to be the slowest in the war so far. German resistance was weak and the ridge and trench were taken, the latter being obliterated. The right hand company overshot the mark whilst the left, unable to consolidate the former enemy trenches, dug in behind them. Alas, the fog then lifted, exposing the troops who were sniped and shelled with such accuracy that the Battalion suffered over 100 casualties. But the gains were held and the enemy deprived of their view of the British lines and communications, and now themselves under observation. They also had 200 prisoners and many dead, outnumbering the British losses.

On their return to the line on the 22nd February, the 1st South Staffs found the forward position 1,000 yards in front of Munich Trench. Patrols on the 24th soon confirmed the Germans had withdrawn, and the 91st Brigade were ordered to advance on Serre onto a ridge one and a half miles north of Beaumont Hamel. The attack on Serre was at dawn in thick fog, and although losing touch with neighbouring units, the Staffords drove back enemy rearguards at the point of the bayonet and captured an orchard occupied by German machine gunners. By 9.30am they had reached their objective, and later in the day they had consolidated and regained touch on both flanks. The open fighting had been a welcome change and casualties had been light.

The enemy was determined to make the follow up after their withdrawal as difficult as possible. Villages were demolished, roads cratered, booby traps cunningly laid, and there were well sited rearguards that hindered and endangered the advance. Even so, by the 22nd March, the Battalion was at Puisieux, taken after hard fighting by the 22nd Brigade and the next day there was a 5 mile advance to Courcelles. Here, work was again required on the roads before the invaluable guns could advance.

The 91st Brigade's position was east of St. Leger on the 27th, in preparation to attack Croiselles, an important enemy observation post thought to be lightly held. The attack was on a two battalion front, the South Staffs on the left, and on their right, the 22nd Manchesters. The approach was over a bare exposed ridge. Hindered by the enemy demolitions, the British artillery only gave inadequate support, and when the attack started it was soon obvious the village was strongly held by a determined enemy. Enemy machine guns and riflemen, who were little worried by British artillery, caused many casualties, but did not stop the two units pressing on with grim determination. The Staffords right forward company reached the uncut wire at the edge of Croiselles, but could advance no further and withdrew to a sunken road, where it endured sharp shelling and drove off a strong German counter-attack. The left company were more unfortunate, under machine gun fire from the start, until pinned down by deadly fire from the flank. Isolated, its left exposed, and a gap between it and the other company, it was fiercely attacked, soon out flanked and surrounded. After gallant resistance with many killed or captured only the left platoon escaped.

Well under strength to start with these additional 134 casualties were serious. They were relieved on the night of 28th/29th March, and they went back smarting from their defeat. Three days later the 91st Brigade was again ordered to attack Croiselles, but now more was done to ensure success. More troops were used, and as the artillery could get closer, better support was available. Again the Staffords had a prominant part, two companies forward to the right of the Brigade, with the 9th Devons of the 20th Brigade on their right, on their left the 21st Manchesters, and beyond them the Queens. The objective was a railway embankment and cutting between Croiselles and the hamlet of Ecoust to the south east. At 5.15am on the 2nd April the attack started under a creeping barrage and, with slight loss, took the first objective and a few prisoners; the remainder of the defenders making for the Hindenburg line, though being badly shot up by small arms fire en route.

A First World War British Mills grenade

About 5.45am the support company passed through on its attack on the second objective, preceded by the barrage, but finding no troops on their flanks sent back for orders, to be told to push on which they sucessfully did. A few hours later, touch was gained on the flanks and the positions consolidated and firmly held. The South Staffs could claim an advance of 1 mile, severe loss to the enemy, with only 27 wounded and their revenge for the previous setback. After this engagement the Staffords withdrew to Puisieux to work on roads and railways.

The 2nd Division had a long period of training in the rear after the Somme, going back into the trenches in late January 1917, and taking over a sector south and east of Ancre. On the 25th January, the 2nd South Staffs were in trenches near Courcelette, to the left of the Division front, and easily beat off an attack following a night of bombing and shelling. Following this, and on relief, practice attacks were made on representations of enemy trenches and forming up at night.

The looming attack was to be on the high ground of the upper Ancre valley and south of the villages of Miraumont and Pys, a pronounced salient jutting into the British line. Two divisions, the 2nd and 18th, had the primary role, the 63rd a subsidiary one. Zero hour was at 5.45am on the 17th February, but without a preliminary barrage, to save tearing up the ground. The weather helped the Germans, the rapid thaw the night before turning the hard ground into sticky mud. A bombardment of the British trenches and rear positions and numerous flares sent up by the enemy showed it was no surprise, it was later learnt that the enemy was expecting this attack and had been strongly reinforced.

The 2nd South Staffs in the 6th Brigade attack were most unfortunate. As the three forward companies left the trenches they were swept by a hail of fire and, although that on the right reached its objective, the others were forced back and without their support its situation was hopeless and it too withdrew. Of ten officers who went over the top only one came back unscathed, and over 100 other ranks were casualties. The road improvements now became so important that training had to be neglected. The troops were exposed to continual shelling, on 8th March, 21 in one company were hit. On 13th March, the Battalion moved up, two days later holding the Brigade front near Achiet le Grand. The enemy trenches opposite at Bihucourt, 2 miles north west of Bapaume, were reported to be evacuated, but fighting patrols sent out to investigate were fired on and withdrew, leaving an observation post between the lines. On the misty morning of the 16th the enemy could be seen working hard on their trenches and wire, a normal ruse before retiring. A Lewis gun was cautiously sent out and gave one such party an unpleasant surprise.

The next day the big enemy retreat was a fact, its extent evident by the smoke from burning villages, and the explosions as roads were cratered. The wanton destruction of immature fruit trees and other non-military damage was further proof of the inherent spitefulness of the Boche.

The 2nd Division, with the King's and a company of the Staffords as advance guard, followed up and two companies, also of the Staffords, occupied positions covering the move that was almost unopposed. It took the Division nearly 10 miles beyond their former lines. On the 19th March the Division retraced their steps on transfer from the 5th to the 13th Corps, spending a month in training and road work.

The 1st British offensive of 1917 was the battle of Arras in April, and to achieve surprise it was decided to launch a series of small "Chinese" attacks at different places. The 2nd South Staffs moved to forward trenches 6 miles north east of Arras, opposite the Hindenburg Line at Oppy, on the 18th April. Dawes, the C.O., was one of the wounded during 4 days of continuous shelling. A feint attack by the King's preceded the real assault on Oppy Wood and village, on the 28th.

The Battalion was split, with a strong company attached to the Essex, another to the Middlesex, the remainder used as carrying parties. The 6th Brigade were to cover 1,200 yards and attack, followed up by a barrage, and started at 4.25am. The 5th Brigade and Canadians on the left made good progress, but the 63rd Division to the right were held up by enemy wire. In the meantime the 6th Brigade advanced through the wood despite intense machine gun fire to Oppy, but were strongly counter-attacked from the rear and right and forced to withdraw to their starting line, the target of a crash barrage. The enemy defences were too strong for the British artillery and by manning these with numerous machine guns, the bulk of the German infantry managed to keep out of the shelling until the counter-attack.

Though a third of the Staffords were not involved, there were over 200 casualties, those of the forward units even greater. The 2nd Division strength was further reduced by an unsuccessful attack by the 99th Brigade on the 29th April. Over the next few days the Division reformed as a weak, composite Brigade, the Staffords, King's and Essex making up B Battalion. Another attack on Oppy was planned for 3rd May, this time another division attacking the Wood and village, with B and C Battalions advancing to their left.

The night of the 3rd May was bright and moonlit, but as the troops assembled, British artillery unwisely shot up the German trenches and drew immediate retaliation from the enemy, bringing heavy fire on the assembled troops and approaches, causing losses and delay. The shelling increased as zero, 3.45am, approached, being most intense around B Battalion.

This was formed with two companies of the King's leading, the Essex in support on the left and the Staffords on the right with C Battalion to the left of B Battalion. C took their objectives without much difficulty, but B failed to take Oppy. Again the counter-attackers came from the wood and village. The two support companies had arrived late on their starting lines, the guides having lost their way. When they did advance both Essex and Staffords came under such heavy fire they could not help the King's, who fought gallantly to hold their ground. Having exhausted their grenades they retired onto the support companies.

The Battalion, reorganised and with 400 men, was the strongest in the Division. The Division urgently needed rest and reinforcement, and it had been unlucky - other formations had captured many prisoners, much material and some ground. But it did not get the needed break, spending the next 6 weeks on many tasks including a new line facing the Germans at Arleux and Oppy. On 20th June it transferred from the 13th to the 11th Corps, moving to Bethune. The poor state of morale in the French Army was the reason for the numerous British offensives during 1917.

The Hindenburg line was to be attacked again and the choice of Bullecourt was unfortunate. This strongpoint was 3 miles east of Croiselles, held by picked German troops, and well supported by artillery. The front was too narrow, preventing the British from manouevre and allowing the mass of enemy guns to be concentrated in a small area. The initial attack on the 3rd May, in which the 7th Divison were not engaged, saw the Australians breach the Hindenburg Line to the south, though Bullecourt was not taken. Because of the heavy casualties in this frontal assault against Bullecourt, it was decided the next would be from the south, where the breach had been extended.

42536 Private WALTER SMITH
4th Battalion South Staffordshire Regiment
Killed In Action 12th June 1918

The Death plaque and pair to Pte. Walter Smith of the South Staffordshire Regiment.

On 10th May the 1st South Staffs moved up under continual shelling, with inevitable casualties. The attack by the 91st Brigade started at 3.40am on the 12th, the Staffords on the left and the Queens on the right. They started from trenches thickly strewn with dead from the previous attack, which did nothing to sustain their morale. The Queen's escaped the worst of the enemy barrage and took their objective, as did the right company of the Staffords after considerable loss. Thus most of the village was taken and held. But the left company front were subject to such a hail of machine gun and artillery fire that little progress was made; the reserve also being pinned down at about 9am. At 12am three companies of the 22nd Manchesters came to assist but could not even deploy for the intense machine gun fire.

Throughout the 13th, both units tried to bomb their way forward, being repulsed time after time; one reason being the superior range of the German egg bomb over the Mills. That night the Battalion were due for relief by the Honourable Artillery Company, but in the event the Staffords had to endure another hard day's fighting, not leaving until the next night. On the right, numerous attacks by the Germans were beaten off, and further attacks by the 7th Division on the left, had no success, being withdrawn on the 16th, the failure attributed to lack of artillery due to faulty communications. The Battalion had 180 casualties and there is little doubt the enemy machine gunners could not have done their deadly work so well had they been under constant shelling.

Summer 1917 saw the Germans build a large number of concrete machine gun emplacements known as 'pill boxes'. These were normally half buried and proof against anything except a direct hit by a heavy gun. Being well camouflaged they were difficult to locate and were most formidable defences.

The 1st South Staffs, after a month behind the lines, returned to the trenches in the Bullecourt sector on the 22nd June, to find them too shallow to protect against enemy snipers. Duties were arduous, as the unit were well below strength, but the trenches were soon deepened and a fierce "hate" turned on the snipers. A big raid on July 14th was betrayed by a weak and futile bombardment, and no prisoners were taken in compensation for the casualties. About a week later the emeny supplied much needed information when storm troops raided the Battalion, an officer was wounded and the Germans hustled back to their lines. The enemy officer was apparently boastful and indiscreet.

The British High Command decided the Ypres Salient was to see the next big push; the first two battles had been defensive, this time it would be attack. The 7th Division moved north at the end of August, detraining near Poperinghe on the 30th. But instead of going straight into action the Division remained in the rear, training for a month, bad weather postponing the offensive. Twelve divisions, on a 20 mile front, were to attack with a slight superiority in numbers and a great one in guns. But vile weather and the state of the ground favoured the Germans, the intense fighting having given the whole Salient a desolation particularly its own. Roads had been destroyed, the only approach over duck boards laid on the slimy treacherous mud into which many sank, never to be seen again. The constant shelling had smashed all ditches and drains and the area was one vast, terrible swamp.

Casualties were received by the 1st South Staffs on the 30th August, behind the line at Huberthoek, near Dickebusch, when a bombing raid from the air killed and wounded 29, including two valuable CSMs. Two days later moving forward to take up positions to attack

First World War British signal flare pistol

Polygon Wood, 3 miles east of Ypres, they had a worse experience. They were on a duckboard track, through what had been Inverness Copse, when the quiet was shattered by an appalling artillery concentration, that even the old soldiers accustomed to heavy shelling, agreed was the worst they had ever known. Further progress was impossible, cover being taken in the muddy shell holes for 45 long minutes, when the bombardment stopped as abruptly as it had started. The Staffords moved on leaving 80 dead and wounded behind.

This sector on the edge of Polygon Wood was only distinguishable by shattered tree stumps. In front, the flat desolate ground was dotted with pill boxes and innumerable shell holes, manned by the concealed enemy. The assault was on the morning of the 4th October, with the 91st Brigade, to the right of the Division, and the Staffords to assault the first objective, the 'Red Line'. At 6am the huge British bombardment started, the troops slowly advancing under its cover. Many Germans were hidden in shell holes covered with brushwood to escape air observation, and were promptly captured or killed by Stafford bayonets. The attack had preceded an enemy one by only 10 minutes and the enemy trenches, full of troops, had the full effect of the barrage with severe loss and demoralization of the survivors. Despite this, the Staffords were shot up by machine guns, until these were engaged by Vickers in the second wave and later by the Division on the right in whose area they were sited.

The 'Red Line' was taken and consolidated when the 22nd Manchesters passed through. After hard fighting the 'Blue Line' was also occupied. However the 21st Division had not kept up with the 7th and were well behind. A defensive flank was formed by the Queens who had been in reserve reinforcing the flank. The enemy, however, had suffered too heavily to counter-attack, confining themselves to heavy shelling that night. The next day machine guns and snipers joined in to take their toll of the men in the makeshift trenches. The 6th October proved quieter, and the Staffords were relieved that night. In the C.O.s report, Beauman states his unit advanced 900 yards on a 450 yard front, killed about 150 enemy troops and captured 90 prisoners - others were poached! It had taken three machine guns and six medium mortars. The Germans for once admitted enormous casualties. But the Battalion had lost over 300.

The 2nd South Staffs were in the Givenchy La Bassee sector from the 20th June to the 6th October and during the 3rd Battle of Ypres there was considerable activity to prevent the Germans reinforcing their hard pressed forces in the Salient The Battalion averaged about 600, the drafts just about replacing the casualties and sick, and increasing at the end of July. Gas was used by both sides but its effects were doubtful. On one occassion 100 gas shells fell on the Staffords area causing two minor casualties; on another a heavy concentration of 112 tons from the 2nd Division's front was, judging from the enemy's feeble reaction, only partially effective.

The Western Front was of grave concern to the British High Command towards the end of 1917. Little reliance could be as yet put on much of the French Army, and Russia was virtually out of the war. The Germans could now transfer huge amounts of veteran troops to France and Flanders. Italy's intervention in 1915 for the Allies, had in effect so far done more harm than good, and though America had declared war on Germany, no more than token forces would be available until well into 1918. The British High Command were aware an enormous enemy offensive was planned for the spring and to hinder this and encourage the French they were forced to use their own weary and depleted troops.

The 3rd Battle of Ypres forced the enemy to weaken other sectors. The place selected for attack was the Cambrai sector near the centre of the front the British held. Here the large number of intended tanks could be concealed, and the ground suited their use. The Germans combined the Hindenburg and Siegfried Lines into fomidable fortifications, and behind these an almost equally strong reserve defence system. The 2nd Division had moved to this sector and was in reserve during the attack of 20th November, when the tanks made a sensational breakthrough, that could not be exploited for lack of reserves, shortage of fuel and the exhausted state of the following infantry. The 2nd Division was ordered to relieve the depleted 36th Division at short notice on the 26th November.

A snow storm had converted the trenches into slimy ditches as the troops moved forward in the pitch black. No time had been allowed for reconnaissance and at dawn on the 27th, two brigades were in the trenches, with the 6th on the left and the 99th to the right. The 6th had the 17th Middlesex and 2nd South Staffs in front, with the Kings and Essex in support. The line faced north extending from Bourlon Wood to Moeuvres, crossing the Canal du Nord, a tank obstacle and break in the line of trenches. From the 27th to the 29th, increasing enemy artillery fire and movement indicated an attack was soon to be launched, so the two forward units strengthened their wire until relieved by the support units on the 29th November.

The attack came the next morning with a vicious bombardment including gas shells. Helped by fog the enemy took Canal Lock No. 5 in the Essex sector and the Staffords moved forward west of the canal on a three company front to meet this threat. Observers reported the whole of the Division front was thick with enemy infantry, being particularly strong in front of Moeuvres and on the right, where the 2nd Division linked with the 47th. An S.O.S. was followed swiftly by accurate shellfire that tore gaps in the massed enemy infantry, but these fiercely pressed on until they met the small arms fire of the defenders, who had not had such targets since the beginning of the war and fired until their rifles were too hot to hold. The deep, wide and empty canal made a dangerous gap in the line and also for the enemy. To cross it entailed a slide down a slippery brick wall of 20ft and then a climb up the other side by ropes, all this under enfilade fire.

Before noon it was obvious matters were not going well for the defenders; the two forward companies of the Kings had been pushed back by sheer weight of numbers, until bombers, assisted by A Company of the Staffords, partially restored the situation. The Essex company had lost No. 5 Lock after heroic resistance, and 'B' company, moving up to its aid along Canal Trench, had to pass through two enemy barrages before finding the Essex survivors. Together they forced back the enemy along the trench until exhausting their grenades; they then blocked and held the trench and launching two separate local counter attacks, forcing the enemy still further back and inflicting many casualties. That night, 30th November, the Essex were withdrawn and 'B' continued to hold the block until the next night, when it was relieved itself and used to bring up grenades.

'C' Company came under the command of the 1st King's at 11am and took a full part in the stubborn resistance against strong and repeated attacks throughout the 30th. Early next morning it joined with 'A' and two platoons of the Middlesex, in a bombing raid with mortar support. The unit made good progress forming a defensive flank against continual bombing attacks, under cover of machine gun fire, until midnight on the 1st December, when the H.L.I. took over. 'C' again reinforced the line on the 3rd, but was not heavily involved.

'D' provided carrying parties for the King's on the 1st day. The next day it went up the Canal Trench, later supporting and then relieving a company of the H.L.I. It withstood several attacks, until the 3rd, when the whole unit went into Divisional reserve. 117 casualties were not unduly heavy in view of the fierce fighting, but as companies of the Battalion were used piecemeal, a clear picture of this battle of Cambrai is not easy. Both defenders and prisoners testify to the enormous losses of the enemy, who repeatedly counter-attacked with great courage and unexpected rapidity.

On December 7th, British troops withdrew from the Siegfried Line to new hastily prepared positions, and this short, difficult retreat was well done. Powerful booby traps caused some loss to the enemy and much gratification to our troops, who had suffered from these in the past. There were again bitter complaints about rear accomodation, some of these being tents without floorboards, poor shelter against the very cold and wet weather. The 2nd Battalion had 70 men admitted to hospital in December.

In January 1918 the 2nd South Staffs received strong and welcome reinforcements, as the fighting south of the Bapaume sector had been costly. Raids on the enemy trenches had revealed many German divisions that had come from the Eastern Front, and speculation grew as to where and when the expected attacks would come.

The enemy plan was to drive a wedge between the British and French forcing the British

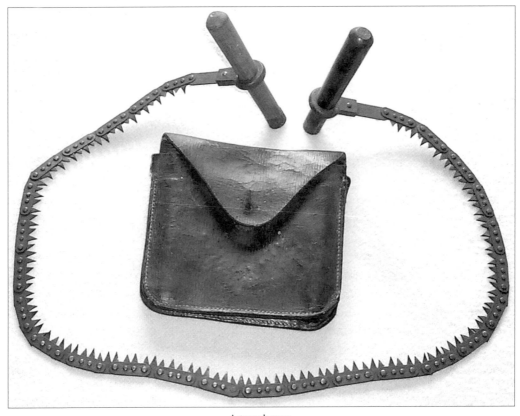

A trench saw

towards the coast. The offensive was to be on a wide 30 mile front from Arras to the Somme by 76 divisions, with between 20-30 batteries of artillery per kilometre. The British would have only 34 Divisions and far fewer guns. The Germans had many advantages, and were without many commitments other than the Western Front. The British were fighting the Turks in Palestine and Iraq, the Austrians in Italy and the Bulgarians in Salonica. In France the ground behind the Germans had seen little if any fighting, their communications were excellent, and the troops behind the trenches were billeted in brick buildings in the undamaged towns and villages. Behind the British lines was unbelievable devastation from the prolonged fighting - and it was terrain with which the Germans were familiar.

All available British troops were involved in improving communications in early 1918. The other problem was the lack of reserves to stem the inevitable enemy breakthrough. The German High Command was obviously gambling heavily on this offensive, for the trickle of American troops was rising to a flood and it was realised that if the war was to be won it must be before these forces were able to render assistance to the hard pressed British and French.

The enemy attack on 21st March was preceded by an intense mustard gas bombardment on the British trenches and communications for several days, causing cruel loss. The weather favoured the Germans, a thick mist allowing unobserved troop concentrations and assisting their advance, besides hindering the dispersion of the mustard gas. The thick mist severely handicapped the defenders, especially the artillery that could do little to help the outnumbered infantry, the enemy guns firing on fixed lines at known ranges were hardly affected.

The 2nd Division, in reserve at Rocquigny, 5 miles south east of Bapaume, heard the noise as the massed enemy artillery pounded the forward British positions. The enemy hidden in the mist and unscathed, swept on silencing the outposts and then assaulting the main defences, many of the sub units fighting to the last man. On the afternoon of the 22nd, the 2nd South Staffs moved to the 'Green Line', left of the 5th Corps front, the

First World War .303 SMLE, the brass butt plate indicating it belonged to the 4th Battalion the South Staffordshire Regiment

Cheshires of the 19th Division to their left, and the King's on their right. The line was the rearmost and incomplete, and only 3 feet deep. Though shelling and gas had reduced the Battalion strength to 550 it was the strongest of the Division. Alarming rumours were coming in of large enemy advances on many parts of the front.

The Staffords were sharply shelled in the night, and on the 23rd March, stragglers were used to reinforce the thinly held line, that, in the confusion, was the target of our own guns as well as enemy mortars. Reports at dusk said the enemy was massing behind a wood to the front, and at 8.50am on the 24th a heavy barrage hit the line, and a strong attack on the Cheshires was made, when it lifted.

The situation was restored by a counter-attack involving a platoon of Staffords from 'C' Company. A much larger attack forced back the defenders on both sides of the 6th Brigade, and the forward companies were ordered to retire to Battalion H.Q. under covering fire from the reserves. 'C', following the Cheshires, were overwhelmed and anihilated. 'A', fighting doggedly, waited too long and only a few survivors returned to tell of a last gallant stand. The other two companies reached H.Q. in good order, though hard pressed. C.O. Alban was twice wounded and narrowly escaped capture.

The 2nd Division's *History,* on page 567, headed *"The Gallant South Staffords"* records: *"Never throughout the four years of war which had gone before, had the Gallant South Staffords proved themselves such stout soldiers as on 24th March 1918."*

The retreat was covered by the Machine Gun Corps, and though forced back nearly everywhere, they inflicted severe losses as they withdrew. Continuing their retreat the remnants of the Battalion took up positions at Beaulencourt, south of Bapaume, but the Germans relentlessly pressed on and the tired troops were forced back to Flers, over the Somme and across the Bapaume to Albert road. In a few days the British had lost all the ground they had taken with great loss. On the 25th March the Battalion could only muster four officers, including the M.O., and 80 odd men.

The same day a weak company of worn out men marched back to Ancre taking up positions behind Hamel in a support role, and on the 26th a few small detachments from the Tank Corps, some stragglers and three Lewis guns strengthened the Battalion, which spent the next few days by the Ancre or close to it. Significantly the period was spent in much the same area and hopes rose that the enemy thrust had fizzled out. At the end of the month the unit had 9 officers and 387 other ranks, its reserve having rejoined, but reinforcements for the Division were not allocated to regiments but into a composite battalion, to get them into action with the least delay. On the 30th the King's and Staffords, under a C.O. from the King's, withdrew to Hedauville , north west of Albert, for much needed rest.

The casualty list was then assessed, this being difficult with two companies almost being obliterated, the missing being recorded as 10 officers and 341 other ranks. It was not known how many were still alive, but 'A' Company had fought nearly to the last man and 'C' did not surrender until most had been killed or wounded. The other companies had lost 144, nine of which were officers.

Summer 1918 saw a trickle of reinforcements from other fronts and, though having little knowledge of trench warfare, they were otherwise well trained. The French Army had much improved and the increasing arrival of American troops inspired the Allies with fresh confidence. Things were starting to go badly for the Germans; their civilians were complaining bitterly because of insufficient and poor food. Though most of the army still fought stubbornly, some units were losing their enthusiasm, and there was grave discontent and even disorder amongst the naval crews. Germany's allies were unreliable and longing for the war to end.

By May, the 2nd South Staffs were in the trenches south of Arras or training in the rear. In June there were raids by both sides, but in July, enemy raids decreased, the British on this front now having complete supremacy in No Man's Land. That month, the 6th Brigade were holding the trenches at Ayette, 7 miles south of Arras, and apart from heavy gas shelling, the situation was reasonably quiet, until the 2nd battle of Arras started on the 21st August.

The 1918 battle of Arras was the British attempt to break through the enemy line following an important French sucess in July. On the 21st August, the 99th Brigade took its objectives, and the 6th Brigade went forward for the next phase, the taking of Ervillers, 4 miles north of Bapaume. Forming up north east of Courcelles, with the Kings on the left and the Staffords on the right, and for the first time supported by tanks - each forward unit having three, the advance started at 11am, on a two company front for each Battalion, and advancing quickly through the enemy's barrage. A few troublesome machine guns were overrun by the tanks and by 12.30 the first objectives west of Ervillers had been taken, and the area mopped up by the rear companies. The left Stafford company came under heavy machine gun fire but Lewis guns replied with such effect that 30 gunners were killed or captured. The right hand company also accounted for 20 machine guns, helping to take the village and depriving the Germans of many of its picked men.

The artillery bombarded Ervillers until it was almost surrounded by the leading companies, who entered as soon as the barrage lifted. The enemy fought fiercely, but the attackers soon cleared the village, taking many prisoners and an assortment of guns. More were captured by the rear companies and by dusk an outpost line was established. The Battalion finally accounted for 500 prisoners, 14 guns and howitzers and 52 machine guns. The 189 casualties were not excessive in view of this important victory. The large number of prisoners and weapons captured indicated a weakening of enemy resistance - they now preferred to surrender rather than fight to the finish. As a result of the August offensives the enemy were driven back to the Hindenburg Line - the next and formidable British objective.

A contemporary First World War trench cap, the South Staffordshire Regiment

The 6th Brigade was relieved for a week and assembled on the 2nd September for an assault on the high ground west and south west of Morchies, 6 miles east of Ervillers, as a start to the second battle of Cambrai. With two companies forward, the 2nd Battalion advanced on the Brigade right, and after an accurate barrage, resistance was so slight the first objective had fallen within 15 minutes. Before it could be consolidated orders came to continue, and accompanied by cavalry and "Whippet" tanks, the Brigade went forward another 5 miles. By dusk they were east of the villages of Demicourt and Hermies and near the Canal du Nord. The old 80th had been fortunate in having few casualties for such a big advance.

The next three weeks, in or out of the trenches, were uneventful whilst preparations were made to assault the Canal. The Brigade formed up at Doignies, west of Demicourt, on 26th September and that night the British guns opened a terrific barrage on the enemy trenches and supply lines. Other troops had secured the Canal du Nord and, with the King's and South Staffs leading, the 6th Brigade moved south east of Flesquieres, 6 miles south west of Cambrai. The two leading units were then ordered on to Orival Wood via the east of the village. As the Battalion skirted Flesquieres it came under heavy machine gun fire from the wood and Graincourt to the north and was forced to shelter in trenches north of the village until an attack could be organised. At 2.00am troops on the left of the Brigade attacked Graincourt and took it at about 3.30am. The Staffords and Kings successfully attacked Orival Wood two hours later.

A further advance ordered on the Graincourt Line, east of the village, had to be abandoned because of the strong enemy resistance. The attackers took a temporary line for the night. The Battalion casualties were about 100 of all ranks. Amongst the prisoners taken was a German regimental commander who was indignant at being taken away by a soldier and demanded an officer escort! On the night of the 27th September, the objectives for the next day were announced as the trenches covering the Canal de l'Escaut, the crossing of the canal and a support line covering it from the east.

At 5.15am the next morning the attack resumed with a creeping barrage, 10 minutes ahead of the infantry. With two companies forward, the Staffords had the 99th Brigade on their left and the Kings on the right, and up to the canal the advance went so well that the Battalion captured an 8" and a 4.2" howitzer, 4 field guns and many machine guns and mortars, with over 300 prisoners, mostly from the German Navy, indicating the growing shortage of manpower and the impotence of the High Seas Fleet. On the west bank of the canal was an embankment, and when the forward companies tried to leave, they were pinned down by machine gun fire, and dug in until relieved by the 17th Royal Fusiliers. Casualties of about 170 were sustained and on the 29th another 30 were added when the 2nd South Staffs were viciously shelled at Noyelles.

The first crossing of the canal was by other formations and when the 6th Brigade moved into the line, on the 3rd October, it was east of the waterway and south of Cambrai, still held by the enemy. Big fires in the town a few days later were signs of the German evacuation. Ten days later the 2nd Battalion occupied Niergnies, 2 miles south of Cambrai, now in British possession, and were billeted in houses left in a state of filth by the enemy. Training included ceremonial parades, so there could no longer have been danger from hostile aircraft. A great advance continued on every sector of the front and when the 2nd Division moved now it was across ground held by the enemy continually since 1914. The Staffords were at St. Hilaire, 8 miles east of Cambrai, on 23rd October, taking over trenches north of Quesnoy on the 27th. In this advance there were casualties from long distance shelling, but the speed of the enemy retreat stopped the usual desolation - the villages were almost intact and billets were good, and there is no mention in the war diary of booby traps.

The Battalion suffered its last casualties in support at Quesnoy and it was then employed on essential road work. Meanwhile it was obvious the German army was disintegrating and rumours of the impending armistice were prevalent. On the 10th November British troops were in Mons, the Staffords about 15 miles south. The arrogance of the original German terms were quickly modified by Foch's uncompromising refusal, and at 11am on the 11th there was a cessation of hostilities. The 2nd Battalion finished the war close to where it started, four long years before, having endured much to gain its 28 battle honours. It had been engaged in many of the fiercest battles on the Western Front and suffered enormous casualties, but never lost its fighting spirit. It was fortunate in remaining in the same brigade and division throughout the war, and if the latter was almost consistently unlucky this in no way detracted from its reputation, which in France was very high, although at home little was known of it.

The advantages expected from Italy's declaration of war on Austria and Germany, in 1915, did not happen, and the sensational victory at Caporetto in October 1917 laid all Italy open to the Austrians, who had considerable German assistance. So critical was the situation that British and French Divisions were rushed from the Western Front, where every man was desperately needed to bolster up the Italians.

The 1st South Staffs left Anvin, near St Pol, on the 10th November 1917, complete with transport, in two trains, and after a slow, uncomfortable, but interesting journey, detrained at Legnago, east of Mantua, on the 25th. They received a rapturous welcome, but the local rations of crushed beans were even refused by the horses, let alone the troops. With its usual efficiency the Army Service Corps was providing normal food within a couple of days. The arrival of these

The Distinguished Conduct Medal of Cpl. Thomas

efficient, well equipped men heartened the Italian army, that then stabilised a front along the River Piave north of Venice. After strenuous marching the 7th Division helped construct a reserve line around Vicenza, and this was followed by intensive training for the new drafts.

The 21st December saw the Battalion at Crespano, at the foot of the Alps, digging trenches to cover a retreat from the forward positions in the mountains. About the middle of January 1918 the Division took a portion of the line, and eventually the Staffords were in trenches on the Montello Hill overlooking the Piave. The river between the opposing forces was a formidable obstacle about half a mile wide, with a swift current of icy water, shifting channels and white shingle that betrayed movements at night. Helped by spotter planes, artillery shelled each others trenches and infantry work was confined to patrols, that on the British side tried unsuccessfully to cross the river, though a little information regarding the enemy positions was gained. After the Western Front, conditions were rather like uncomfortable peace time manoeuvres and the Austrian shelling caused very few casualties.

Early in March, with the new German offensive, sudden orders came to return to France, one brigade actually entraining before the orders were cancelled. This was a break however from the not very exciting trench life, and by the 8th the Staffords were at Villafranca south of Verona, where training included mountain warfare, and the Battalion won the Divisonal Football cup, beating one unit 17-2!

The next move was to the Asiago Plateau, reached after several days march and a bus ride up the steepest portion. With forests on the many hills and views of snow capped mountains in the distance, the scene was very different from the dreary mud flats of Flanders.

When the Staffords went into the line in March, the enemy were 2,000 yards away, too far for Beauman, who immediately started active patrolling, a practice much disliked by the Austrians. A very successful raid was carried out by the Battalion on an outpost in a ruined farm, Vaisteter, by two companies under Capt. Kendrick. In half moon formation they crept so quietly they got within 150 yards of their objective undetected, despite a bright moon. As they waited, British howitzers crashed on the farm and when they stopped, the centre rushed the buildings, under fire from rifle grenades, while the flanks surrounded the farm. The Austrians replied wildly, but the farm taken with a loss of only 5 wounded, whilst the 40 defenders were either killed or captured. This brilliant, little affair received much favourable attention and Kendrick was awarded a well deserved bar to his M.C.

The 91st Brigade spent over 3 months on the Asiago Plateau, with persistent rumours that the Division was to return to the Western Front, where the tide of war was turning for the Allies. In June the Austrians launched an offensive, which had partial sucess. The 91st Brigade, in reserve, and prepared to counter-attack, received some casualties from shell fire. The forward troops retrieved their trenches with little difficulty and required no assistance.

In July numerous Austrian deserters came in reporting that a large withdrawal was imminent. To test this, the Division carried out four raids almost simultaneously. The Staffords were to attack Canove and Bellochio on the night of the 8/9th August; the former, a large village, well wired and strongly held, and as it had been raided before, the garrison was very alert. There was no time to practice the raid, and it was the hardest task of the four planned.

At midnight, the forward companies advanced and soon reached the wire, mostly intact. Seeking gaps they came under enfilade machine gun and small arms fire from the trenches, but gaps were found and the enemy, who put up stiff resistance, were forced back. Reinforced by the support companies, the Staffords rushed the village, until at the far end a pill box enfiladed the street and stopped any further advance towards Bellochio on the left. The CO decided to leave the second objective and to complete the mopping up of Canove. The Battalion brought back a number of prisoners and killed many of the enemy, but its own casualties of over 60 were the highest of the raids. All ranks fought with great determination - the attack was the first real action for many of those taking part and the only one on the Plateau.

In September the British divisions in Italy were reduced to nine battalions and the 91st Brigade lost the 21st Manchesters. Again orders came for a move to France, and again they were cancelled at the last moment to the regret of most of the officers and men. The greatly improved situation, not only on the Western Front, but in Salonica and in Palestine, led to speculation this may lead to equal sucess in Italy. Rumour said the Piave was to be crossed and for once the rumour was right.

The main attack was to be on the right, by the Italians, who had by far the most men between Feltre and Vittorio Veneto. The centre, which we are concerned with, was to force the Piave north east of Treviso, and on the left an advance was to be made across the Asiago Plateau. It was decided to cross Piave in two stages via an island, Grave di Papadopoli, which was known to be heavily defended. After some fierce fighting by the Honourable Artillery Company and the Royal Welch Fusiliers, the island was securely held by the 25th October. The next day was foggy and a pontoon bridge was built with great skill and courage by the R.E., allowing the 20th and 91st Brigades to cross over a river much swollen by rain.

First World War pair and silver cricket medal, won in Italy in the Great War,
of Pte. Cotterill, the 9th South Staffordshire Regiment.

These two brigades advanced across the ford, each having one battalion forward, that of the 91st being the 22nd Manchesters, with the Staffords in support, and the Queens in reserve. The Austrian defences, visible across the still wide portion of the river, were indeed formidable, with a 10 foot embankment or bund forming the chief obstacle. This was impervious to shell fire and well wired - had it been held by the Germans it may have been impregnable; but the Austrians had not the same resolve and the British were confident of success.

During the night of the 26/27th October, the Austrian wire was bombarded, and early on the 27th the attackers assembled to make the crossing. The frontage of 3,000 yards was too wide for two battalions and another could have been used to advantage. The Manchesters started poorly, coming under heavy fire on entering the water, and finding a swift current, in some places four foot deep, a difficult and dangerous proposition. There was a natural inclination to bunch up and some were swept away. After so many previous disappointments none of the infantry expected the wire to be cut - nor was it. The Manchester C.O. finding his forward companies pinned down, called for the support, and was closely followed by the Staffords. Together, under Lewis gun fire, the units wriggled under the wire and once clear rushed the bund with the bayonet. The Austrians, who probably relied too much on their strong defences, put up but feeble resistance, many not waiting to fight, and those who did were quickly dead or captured.

The C.O.s reorganised their units and continued the advance on a two company front, the Staffords to the left of the Manchesters; and once in position, the Battalion gained touch with the 23rd Division on the left. The crossing of the Piave, in the face of heavy fire from very strong positions, was a noteworthy feat, that could only have been achieved by well trained and disciplined troops full of fight. Arms and ammunition had to be carried across the icy water and it is a wonder that more troops were not lost.

The casualty MM and trio of Acting Colour Sergeant W A Beech, killed in action on the 26/10/1917

The hamlet of Vendrane, close to the bund, was soon cleared by the Staffords, taking 40 prisoners and then advancing through the vineyards to the ruined village of S. Michele di

HE whom this scroll commemorates was numbered among those who, at the call of King and Country, left all that was dear to them, endured hardness, faced danger, and finally passed out of the sight of men by the path of duty and self-sacrifice, giving up their own lives that others might live in freedom.

Let those who come after see to it that his name be not forgotten.

2/Lieut. George Henry Tinkler
South Staffordshire Regt.

The illuminated scroll of Lieut George Henry Tinkler, South Staffordshire Regiment.

Piave, to be met by heavy and accurate machine gun fire. The leading troops returned the fire and, under cover of this, the support company charged from the flank, taking the village, which by now contained many dead enemy soldiers. Another three automatic guns and 60 prisoners were taken. The Battalion reorganised beyond S. Michele and waited for the guns to lift, but its advance was soon checked by a fortified farmhouse which had been missed by the artillery and was covered by outposts. These were driven in, the main buildings were rushed and the occupants were bombed out. Nearby was a dyke filled with dead Austrians, who had been killed by the shell fire.

The village of Tezze was defended desperately, but unavailingly, yielding three field guns, 12 machine guns and 240 Austrian prisoners. By noon all the objectives had been seized and the Battalion was digging in against counter attack, stated to be imminent by the captives. During the day's fighting, the old 38th had captured or killed almost the whole of the Austrian 38th Regiment, whilst sustaining, in their 7th Division, casualties far lighter than expected and out of all comparison to the enemy's, who also lost many hundreds of prisoners. But the rapid infantry advance had begun to out-range the artillery. On the afternoon of 27th October, two batteries crossed the pontoon bridge and moved up to prepare for the counter-attack.

The 7th Division waited for the counter-attack with a justified confidence. The Queens sent up a company to reinforce the Staffords, but these were not required. The Staffords, and other units heavily engaged, had no difficulty driving off the enemy's half hearted assaults.

At a Brigade conference, on the 28th October, it was decided to resume the advance in the same formation. The Staffords objective was the village of Borgo Belussi and on capture, a line was to be dug 1,000 yards forward. Only the Austrian machine gunners resisted; the other infantry had not recovered from their previous mauling and fled. Lewis guns soon put the enemy weapons out of action and the village was cleared with considerable enemy loss and eight automatic guns taken. The forward position was occupied and consolidated.

Fighting patrols went out, and one entered the large village of Vazzola, a mile in front of the line; both Vazzola and Belussi were inhabited by Italians. In the former the patrol found great confusion and a large pack train in the process of being assembled. It helped itself to riding animals and rode back, followed at a respectable distance by Austrian cavalry. Another patrol, however, was held up by accurate machine gun fire. That afternoon the Battalion was relieved and marched to Belussi.

The same night, orders were received to take Vazzola, at which there was deep and heart felt cursing, because the men were tired and hungry - their rations had not arrived and their boots, hardened by the river, could not be taken off with any hope of putting them on again. By midnight the Staffords had reached their former front line and went on towards the village. It was tough going, but the Austrians were in full retreat and it was essential to keep them on the run. Three companies of the Staffords surrounded the village and the other cleared it. If one account is correct, the Austrians were surprised, and their outposts, including the staff officer, were sleeping , and were captured with 47 men, a gun and two machine guns.

At dawn, a mounted patrol rode to the Monticano River, which if properly held could be a formidable obstacle, and from which Vazzola was shelled by the enemy. Ordered to advance across the river, the 91st Brigade had the Queens as an advance guard, followed by the Staffords, who came under heavy fire from machine guns sited in the trees. The advance halted when the Queens were held up on the far side of the Monticano. The Staffords were ordered to give support, and one company moved to the right and forded the river; the other three companies found a bridge and formed up under the river bank.

The Queens were being fired on from the small but strongly held village of Cimetta. Though no reconnaissance was possible, and the view was restricted, orders were given to the company commanders, who acted at once. Under the impromptu, but effective support of two field and one Italian mountain gun, and a pair of machine guns, the Battalion attacked the village with two companies forward. Enemy automatic guns opened intense fire, but it was largely harmless thanks to the forest cover. Two platoons of the right rear company met and promptly engaged a large part of the enemy and took more than their own number of prisoners. Meanwhile the leading companies were opposed by many machine guns, sited well in front of Cimetta, but these were quickly dealt with by the forward sections, who displayed great initiative and courage.

Both battalions now formed up on the outskirts, with the Staffords on the right, and assaulted the village with a grim determination the enemy could not withstand. House after house was cleared and the occupants killed or captured; indeed the number of prisoners became quite embarrassing, the Battalion taking over 700. The 15 machine guns taken were regarded as more important. By 3.15pm, Cimetta had fallen, but there was a gap on the right of the Brigade so the Queens took over the village, and the Staffords occupied the area between Cimetta and the 20th Brigade, and dug in.

Firing died down during the night of the 29th/30th October, and a belated issue of rations and rum cheered up the desperately weary officers and men. A dawn patrol could not make contact with the retreating enemy and at 9am the 22nd Brigade passed through the 91st. At noon the Battalion marched to Roverbasso, overtaken on the way by Italian cavalry and armoured cars. Many Italian flags were flying from the houses and the inhabitants enthusiastically welcomed their liberators. Roverbasso was reached at 8pm and at last the exhausted men could sleep.

Neither the pursuing infantry or the Italian cavalry could catch the fleeing Austrians, who discarded their arms and equipment, but the Royal Flying Corps could, and when the Battalion continued its advance on 2nd November, dead men and animals, abandoned guns and wagons, all testified to the terrible destruction wielded by this comparatively new arm. After a long unopposed march, the unit reached the town of Pordenone, 40 miles north of Venice, finding it wantonly looted and some houses still burning. The next march on the 3rd was a short one; it was an exciting day for there were strong rumours of an impending armistice and the many staff cars going forward convinced the cynical infantry, as nothing else could do, that the fighting had really ceased! The Staffords, less two companies guarding prisoners, had almost reached the River Tagliamento on the 4th November, when news came through that an armistice would come into effect at 3pm.

The Battalion had little time to rejoice, for that night 1,400 prisoners including a divisional commander and nearly 200 officers arrived. A message of congratulations for Lord Cavan and his Command from the King was the first to be read out, and, among the many received by the Battalion, that of General Shoubridge had an endearing simplicity. *"I am too much an old friend of the South Staffords to send them a formal message of congratulation,*

Four official photographs taken on the British Italian Front, with men of the 1st Battalion South Staffordshire, 7th Division, 91st Brigade constructing trenches

Note the Staffordshire Knot painted on the soldier's helmet

Possibly taken on 21 December, 1917, when the 1st Battalion South Staffords were at Crespano
at the foot of the Alps, digging trenches to cover a retreat from forward positions in the mountains

The Italian Alps are seen in the background, totally unlike views of the Western Front.
Men of the 1st Battalion South Staffordshire are digging trenches

but tell them I always expected great things of the Staffords, but they always exceeded even my expectations. I congratulate everyone most heartily".

There is little to record of the 1st Battalion's last 4 months in Italy; it assembled near Vicenza and as there were few regular soldiers left in its ranks, demobilization rapidly thinned them. It was a difficult time for the Army as the average man just could not understand the necessity for keeping him in it once the war was over. Fortunately the authorities tackled the problem sensibly and promptly. The method of release was carefully explained and educational schemes, and military and recreational training, as well as the mens' desire not to let the unit down, kept them out of mischief. In Italy the non fraternization order did not apply - and this helped.

Despite its very heavy losses, the Battalion had not been altogether unfortunate during the war; campaigning in Italy had been far more pleasant than the Western Front. There had been few changes of C.O.s and all were from the Regiment. Draft soldiers, sometimes of unpromising material, were soon told what was expected of them, and even those from outside the county quickly acquired the characteristics of the South Staffords including his accent! Apart from the strong regimental tradition there was a keen pride in belonging to the famous 7th Division

The 3rd and 4th Battalions (1st King's Own Stafford Militia) had belonged to the Special Reserve since 1908. The 3rd did not leave England but trained officers and troops, chiefly for the regular units, at its HQ on the NE Coast around Newcastle. Jersey was the initial war station of the 4th where they remained for two years prior to moving to Redcar in Yorkshire in an anti-invasion role. In October 1917 the 4th went to France, after a short stay in Canterbury, and disbanded in June 1918, after nine months arduous service. Besides recruit training, both Special Reserve battalions had large numbers of young officers in urgent need of instruction. In Jersey, in early 1916, the 4th Battalion had 92 2nd Lieutenants. Some of the NCO teachers had the Egyptian Medal and Khedives Star, and one private, the Zulu War medal. These fine old warriors had been on the reserve far too long to be up to date, and so only taught drill and musketry. Modern warfare was taught by officers wounded at the front. The Special Reserve Battalions did not reform after the war, though they are shown in Army Lists. After nearly three hundred years of faithful, if often broken and unspectacular service, the Stafford Militia, like all good old soldiers, just faded away!

August 1914 saw the 5th and 6th Battalions of Lt-Cols Crawley and Taylor in camp, which eased mobilization. Crawley later handed over to Raymer, whilst Waterhouse, who had already done his full period of command plus an extension, suceeded Taylor. Both were in the 137th (Staffordshire) Brigade of the 46th (North Midland) Division, the first complete Territorial Division to go to France early in March 1915. I give some account of their war service in chapter. 12. Before going overseas the two battalions became the 1/5th and 1/6th, the regular units drawing on the Depot and Special Reserve for reinforcements. The Territorial Force found its reserves from the 2/5th and 2/6th, and, when these prepared for active service, from the 3/5th and 3/6th.

These second line Territorial battalions of Staffordshire formed the 176th Brigade of the 59th Division, a duplicate of the 46th. Before going to France the 59th saw bitter fighting in the Dublin Rebellion of Easter 1916, remaining in Ireland until January 1917 and then to

France via Salisbury Plain. The next month the original CO.s were replaced by Lt-Col Armstrong, 2/5th, and Lt-Col Wortley, 2/6th. The 2/5th disbanded in January 1918 and the draft joining the 3/5th and 3/6th, combined to form the 5th (Reserve) Battalion T.F. in 1917, but did not leave England.

The 7th (Service), 8th (Service) and 9th (Pioneer) Battalions were raised at Lichfield in August and September 1914, as part of what was popularly known as "Kitchener's Army".

The 7th, under Lt-Col Daukes, was in the 33rd Brigade of the 11th Division, fighting in Gallipoli in 1915, and following a period in Egypt, to France in July 1916 where it stayed until the end of the war.

The 8th, under Lt-Col Going, was posted to the 51st Brigade of the 17th Division, and went to France in July 1915, starting trench warfare attached to units of the 137th Brigade on the Ypres Salient. The fierce fighting it endured is shown by the fact that, when it disbanded in February 1918, its killed equalled its original strength.

The 9th started as a Service battalion going to a North Country Division, the 23rd, commanded by Maj-Gen Babington. On the formation of Pioneer units in Divisions, a census was taken of battalions and those with the most suitable men, including the 9th, were chosen. The 23rd Division was among those selected to go to Italy in 1917 and the 9th Battalion remained with it until both disbanded after the war.

The 10th Battalion was raised in November 1914, going to the reserve in April 1915, after amalgamating with the 11th, which had always been on the reserve, and joined the 2nd Reserve Infantry Brigade in September 1916.

The 12th formed as a Labour battalion in July 1916, transferring to the Labour Corps in 1917, so losing its regimental identity, and serving on the Western Front. The 1st Garrison Battalion was raised in January 1917 and served in Bombay; it consisted of unfit men from many regiments being South Staffordshire in name only.

Certain Volunteer units were raised in the County in 1915, to guard vulnerable points, and in 1917, those in the regimental area became Volunteer Battalions, the South Staffordshire Regiment, and wore the badge. In 1918 some were sent as far as the East Coast for guard duties.

Of the many Battle Honours awarded for the war, ten were selected by the Regiment to be borne on the King's colour. They were: MONS, MARNE 1914, AISNE 1914-1918, YPRES 1914-1917, LOOS, SOMME 1916-18, CAMBRAI 1917-1918, ST. QUENTIN CANAL, VITTORIO VENETO (ITALY) and SULVA (GALLIPOLI).

They were won at a terrible cost: 5,999 killed and many more wounded. The heroes of the 1914-1918 War were worthy successors of the gallant old 38th and 80th.

An original and contemporary postcard of the North Staffords camp dated 20th August 1914.

NORTH STAFFS. AUG. 20. 1914.

An early Great War North Stafford Lieutenant's cuff ranked tunic and cap.

Eleven
The History of The Prince of Wales's (North Staffordshire) Regiment during the Great War 1914-1918

A month after the assassination of the Austrian Archduke Franz Ferdinand in Sarajevo, on the 28th June 1914, the major European powers were at war. On 12th August the small British Expeditionary Force began landing in France, following the German invasion of Belgium. Though 18 battalions ultimately wore the knot and plume, and over 4,000 soldiers died with the North Staffords, space limits an attempt to do them all justice, and I will concentrate on the 1st Battalion.

A Great War SMLE rifle* and hooked quillon bayonet, both officially stamped up to the 4th Battalion of the North Staffords.

The 1st North Staffords were in Ireland, and were in the 17th Brigade of the 6th Division, along with the 1st Royal Fusiliers, 2nd Leicesters and 3rd Rifle Brigade, at the outbreak of war. Held in England for fear of invasion for the first three weeks, the Division finally arrived in France on 12th September, after the initial enemy thrust had been stopped and the front had stabilised north of the River Aisne. Here the 1st North Staffords relieved the 2nd South Staffords. Each side in the war now tried to outflank the other in what was known as the 'Race to the Sea'.

The 1st North Staffords stayed ten uneventful days before moving north. From the occasional shelling, patrols and sniper activities, 21 casualties were sustained, and Sergeant Redfern won the Regiment's first DCM in the war, bravely bringing in the body of an officer.

The 6th Division moved to the Armentieres sector of the front in early October. This flat industrial district was in great contrast to the Aisne's rolling countryside. The British met the Germans here in an encounter battle - the line here was yet to be stabilised - and the Staffords captured the village of Outterstene. During this engagement the Battalion only encountered one lone tree in an otherwise featureless landscape, and as nearly every NCO had been trained to indicate targets by finding a 'prominent object', they automatically directed their section's fire towards it. When they reached it, they discovered that the unlocated enemy machine gun that had been holding them up, was in fact sited close by, and its crew were riddled with bullets.

One of the most extraordinary incidents of the war took place at Christmas 1914. On Christmas Eve the Germans opposite started singing, lighting candles and sitting on their parapets. Next, a German soldier, who before the war had been a waiter in Brighton, came to the British lines trying to swop cigars for bully beef. The Stafford company commander asked to be taken to a German officer and as a result there was a truce the next day. It was further agreed that at 10.00 hours both sides could leave their trenches to bury the frozen corpses in their own half of no man's land. In reality it was not long before the boundary line was crossed, British and Germans mingling freely for the rest of the day. The enemy troops were Saxons, who were quick to warn that the unit on their right were Prussians, with a very different attitude to themselves - and the British were not to try to fraternise.

Following this interlude the daily routine of trench warfare resumed. Companies usually did four days in the line and a similar amount in reserve, though considerable danger would still be involved as the reserve providing carrying and working parties. Even at rest out of the line, a battalion would seldom be out of range of enemy artillery. It was often necessary to build up breastworks, and the trenches were often waterlogged in the early days of the war. By the end of January 1915, the Staffords had sustained 502 casualties and had only 5 of their original 24 officers.

Neuve Chappelle was the scene of the first British offensive in 1915, by the First Army. It fell to the Second Army, of which the 6th Division were part, and in which Division the Staffords were serving, to hold the enemy on their front. The Staffords captured the village of L'Epinette for their part, with a pinching operation which was so well planned, it achieved complete surprise and cost few casualties.

In October, the 1st North Staffords were transferred to the 24th Division, a new division which had been badly mauled at the Battle of Loos. With the 8th Royal West Kents, the 8th Queens and the 9th East Surreys, the North Staffords were in the 72nd Brigade, and they served on the Ypres Salient for the next 6 months. Close to Hooge the opposing lines were so close together that the forward saps were separated by the remains of a stable wall. The 1st North Stafford's commanding officer was accompanied by a sergeant who had just rejoined after being wounded in 1914, in visiting his post here. The sergeant bellowed *"Commanding Officer"* at the top of his voice as they approached remembering peace-time procedure. The Germans must have been as astounded as the post's garrison were, at this outburst, when no shower of grenades followed.

In pleasant contrast to the desolation of the Ypres Salient, the 1st North Staffords moved to Wulverghem close to Bailleul. Whilst here the 1st North Staffords suffered two major gas attacks. The first was followed up by enemy infantry, the repulse of which gained the 1st North Staffords a mention in Field-Marshal Haig's despatches. In the second gas attack there was no infantry assault; however there was a second wave of gas shortly after the first that cost the Staffords 31 killed and 134 evacuated, plus an additional 55 caused by the accompanying enemy shell fire.

On the 1st July, the Battle of the Somme, the major British offensive of 1916, began. The 24th Division moved to take its share of the fighting at the start of August. The village of Guillemont was the initial focus for fruitless frontal attacks, but though remaining in this sector for a fortnight the 1st North Staffords did not launch an assault, although if it had not been for Major Dugmore, the commanding officer, forcefully pointing out to the Brigadier that

A contemporary North Stafford silk postcard, produced and sold by local French ladies to the British troops.

Pte G. Harrison of the 7th Battalion North Staffords who was killed in action, 5th April 1916, in Gallipoli.

it would be a futile sacrifice to send them over the same ground, from which two other battalions had already been bloodily repulsed, they would have been too. Despite their not "going over the top", the Staffords still suffered 150 casualties.

Delville Wood was the next place for the 1st North Staffords to go into the line, after a short rest. The 1st North Staffords held part of the NE face,and the 1st South Staffords were to their right at the eastern apex. "Wood" is a misnomer as the trees were just shattered stumps that confused their guides by altering after each bombardment. The ground was a quagmire from continual rain, the trenches were waist deep in liquid mud. But worse of all, 'Devil's Wood' was littered with unburied corpses from six weeks of fighting, the dreadful smell of the decomposing bodies pervading everything.

The Germans launched some strong assaults, covered by a very heavy bombardment, on 31st August Though the 1st North Staffords held firm all day, the units to their left were forced back, causing the Staffords to form a defensive flank. No carrying parties could get forward and the communications were severed. To their right, astride the original German trenches, the South Staffords were under extreme pressure, the North sending over a Lewis machine gun and part of their meagre stock of bombs to try to help. Despite this, eventually, by 7.00pm, the enemy had broken into the South Staffords, forcing them back into the wood and capturing 30 yards of North Stafford trench. 2nd Lieut Worsley earned a bar to his M.C. by preventing further penetration with a hastily established block. The right-hand platoon's commander, 2nd Lieut White, was last seen leading a party of bombers against the Germans, with his revolver in his left hand after his right hand had been shattered. The 1st North Staffords now had both their flanks in trouble. Had they broken, the whole position would have been lost, but they held firm and remained full of fight. Fortunately the German offensive ended.

An attack by the 2nd Queens recaptured the lost stretch of trench the next day. The seven week Battle of Delville Wood officially ended on the 3rd September, and though having cost them 214 men, the Staffords had fought a distinguished part in it.

An interesting footnote - when the Staffords were relieved by the 9th East Surreys, a forward post under a lance-corporal was accidentally left behind. The corporal sent an old soldier back to see what was going on, and to guard against getting shot by the lance-corporal, he bellowed *"what b------s are holding that b---- trench"* and was at once recognised as a Stafford. The lance-corporal still refused to relinquish his position until he had a written order.

After leaving the Somme, the 1st North Staffords moved to Vimy Ridge and then Hulluch in the coalmining area close to Loos. Little of interest happened, other than raids and local engagements - far less popular with the front line troops than the staff. On one occasion, the 1st North Staffords got wind of a German raid near Hulluch and prepared a suitable hot reception. The German commander was manhandled into the Stafford's trench. The company commander asked to see the enemy officer. A very tall Prussian officer caked in mud came down the steps of the company dug-out. After coming smartly to attention, in perfect English he said, *"Gentlemen, I apologise for my appearance but you know what these raids are!"*

Though the 24th Division was involved with the closing stages of the limited but highly successful offensive in June 1917 which captured Messines Ridge SE of Ypres, the 72nd Brigade were in reserve. In preparation for the Third Battle of Ypres the Division moved to the Salient near Zillebeke. In a single week in June, the 1st North Staffords lost their Commanding Officer, Lt. Col Dugmore, and his second in command, both killed by the same shell, and they suffered over 100 other casualties, as the Germans did their best to disrupt the preparations. The next time the 1st North Staffords went into the line, Dugmore's successor was also killed.

From the position from which the Staffords were to launch their attack in the offensive of 31st July, the German lines were approximately 1,000 yards across 'no man's land', though the enemy had forward posts at only 100 yards in places. The initial task for the Staffords was to take Jehovah trench, the German front line, and then advance a further 500 yards to Jordan trench. The remains of Bulgar Wood lay 250 yards beyond this, where it was expected the enemy may counter-attack. The remains of another large wood, Shrewsbury Forest, flanked the line of advance. It was planned for the artillery to blast a way through the German defences for the infantry. There was no possibility of manoeuvre, the advancing Staffords were only able to keep close to the barrage and hope for the best.

Lt. Col V.V. Pope, who was later to become Lt. General, and who landed in France back in 1914 as a junior subaltern, was now in command. Enemy defensive fire had caused a number of casualties before the Staffords 'went over the top' Further casualties, particularly heavy amongst the officers and NCOs, were caused by the stoutly defended forward German posts. The biggest problem came because the unit to the left of the Staffords was not making as much progress, causing the Staffords to suffer badly from enfilade machine-gun fire. Despite this, Jehovah was stormed. Only three officers remained in the three leading companies by now. The

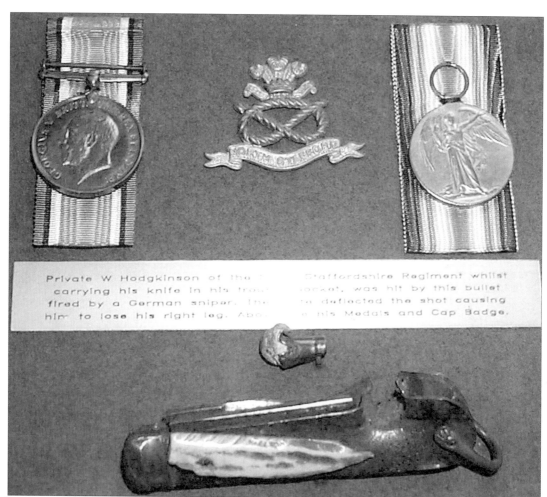

Private W. Hodgkinson of the ... Staffordshire Regiment whilst carrying his knife in his trou... ...ocket, was hit by this bullet fired by a German sniper. Th... ...n deflected the shot causing him to lose his right leg. Abo... ...e his Medals and Cap Badge.

The medals and badge of Private W. Hodgkinson, and his battlefield pocket knife with bullet hole, and the offending German bullet, which caused the loss of his leg whilst serving with the North Staffordshire Regiment in World War I.

North Stafford officer's steel helmet with an officer's bronze cap badge contemporarily attached to it, within a red painted triangle.

1st North Staffords pressed on to Jordan trench, which turned out to be nothing more than a spitlocked line full of water, and one platoon even reached Bulgar Wood.

They were still under enfilading fire from Shrewsbury Forest, and although the 8th Queens to their right had kept up, the unit beyond the Queens had not. The ground around Jordan trench was so waterlogged that digging was impossible - as the Germans had already discovered - so orders were received by both units to return to the Jehovah trench line. The Staffords had lost 11 officers and 258 men, nearly 50% of their strength, but had done all that could be expected of them. The 1st North Staffords earned two MCs, three DCMs and six MMs. They had just reason to be proud of themselves. After the war the anniversary of this attack became the main "Regimental Day".

The 1st North Staffords were now moved to a quiet sector at Hervilly near the Somme, and were not further involved in any serious fighting in the Third Battle of Ypres. They remained there until shortly before the big

Great War officer's sword, engraved J. Foster, 10th N. Staffords.

German offensive of March 1918. On 21st march, the 1st North Staffords were holding a frontage of 2,000 yards, on a slight ridge between Gricourt and Ponruet villages, close to St. Quentin, and along a stream called the Omignon . Their left flank was completely open for about half a mile. The 'red line' main battle position was about 2,000 yards in the rear of the forward positions, near a sunken road. The Essling Redoubt was a rectangular fieldwork, halfway between the two lines. An under-strength battalion was therefore holding a quadrilateral 2,000 yards square. To make things worse, a re-entrant ran from the enemy positions, on the right flank, towards the rear of the Staffords. The reserve battalion from the next division was supposed to block this in the event of an attack. The Staffords had two companies on the outpost line, one in the redoubt and one on the 'red line', with headquarters in the sunken road.

There was a thick mist when the intense and heavy German bombardment, including some gas shells, burst on the Staffords positions, early on 21st March. Soon all communications were severed, and it soon became a soldiers' battle. Using their new infiltration tactics of avoiding defended posts and advancing through gaps, the German infantry penetrated the outpost line at around 9.30am. The forward Stafford companies were quickly overrun, though many posts held out for a long time, and 1st Stafford prisoners were cheered up by seeing large numbers of enemy dead around these. 2nd Lt. Keeble was last seen leading the remnants of his platoon in a desperate bayonet charge against the Germans.

North Stafford badged RSM's pace stick.

The Essling Redoubt came under attack from all sides, the Germans having worked their way along the Omignon. The garrison appear to have fought to the bitter end. Initial attacks on the rear positions close to the sunken road were beaten off, but by 11.30am the Germans from the right worked around to the rear, and were then able to fire down on the Battalion headquarters party, from some mounds behind them. For some time, this unit under Adj. Capt. W. D. Stamer, who had been wounded in the head, managed to hold the enemy off, but as more came on the survivors were obliged to withdraw, and until nightfall, a new position was held a mile back. Two 2nd lieutenants and 21 men comprised the entire Stafford strength in the line at this time. Seldom if ever in its long history had the old 64th struggled more gallantly against overwhelming odds, and with so little glory than on 21st March.

With the addition of transport personnel and odd details, the Staffords were built up into a weak company the next day. Two days later as the retreat continued, the Staffords were again down to two officers and 40 men, and were absorbed into a composite battalion. Falling back fighting, the remnants of the 24th Division distinguished themselves, especially with a stand on the River Avre, until 5th April when the enemy advance came to a halt. '18th March' had cost the 1st North Staffords 19 officers and 662 men.

The 24th Division was now to stay in the quiet Lens sector to the north until the final advance. The trenches here were lined with bricks, and cellars were available as dugouts, the Staffords being located in the remains of a built-up area. The Fourth Army launched the first of a series of limited offensives at Amiens, on 8th August, that sent the Germans reeling back. By the end of September the British were up against the strongly built Hindenburg Line, and the enemy was determined to make a stand here.

It would be October before the 1st North Staffords, under Lt. Col Stamer, who was only 23 years old, were on the move again. They went into action near Cambrai, when the Germans tried to make a stand on the River Selle, but their position was soon penetrated. In the following week's fighting, the Staffords sustained about 200 casualties. The 24th Division advanced some 12 miles in bad weather and along roads methodically destroyed by the enemy.

Following a short rest, they were in action again, although the end was now in sight. In their last 48 hours of fighting the Staffords pushed the Germans back 9 miles in two days - beyond their wildest dreams in the days of the Somme and the Third Ypres.

In the meantime, the 2nd North Staffords were in India. Trouble was ever present on the North West Frontier and it increased when Mohammedan Turkey entered the war. For this reason, nine British battalions were to remain there in an operational role.

Despite being fated to miss the Western Front, the 2nd North Staffords were not inactive. In late 1914 a crisis appeared to be brewing, so they moved from Rawalpindi to Bannu on the Frontier, where they remained for 3 months. There was more serious trouble in 1915, with the Mohmand tribes. The 2nd North Staffords, in the 4th Indian Brigade, along with the 35th Sikh, 30th and 80th Punjabi regiments, moved out against tribesmen near the village of Panjpao on 5th September. Their orders were to create a firing line on a ridge, holding down the enemy as other troops attacked their flanks. This task was successfully achieved, and with the order to retire, they did this so skilfully they stopped the Mohmands from following up.

A month of comparative inactivity followed, and then they were again engaged in a similar action at Panjpao. There was no more fighting after this and on December 2nd, the

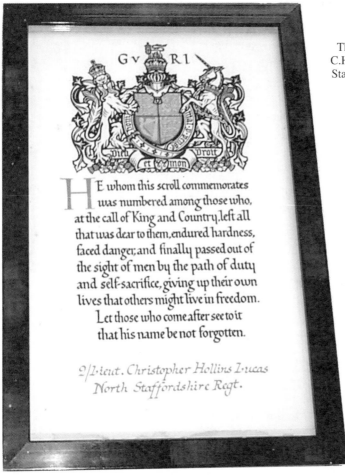

The illuminated scroll of 2nd Lieut,
C.H. Lucas, 8th Battalion of the North
Staffords, who was killed in action on
10th April 1918

GᵛRI

HE whom this scroll commemorates
was numbered among those who,
at the call of King and Country, left all
that was dear to them, endured hardness,
faced danger, and finally passed out of
the sight of men by the path of duty
and self-sacrifice, giving up their own
lives that others might live in freedom.
Let those who come after see to it
that his name be not forgotten.

2/Lieut. Christopher Hollins Lucas
North Staffordshire Regt.

The Distinguished Conduct Medal
trio of 6286 Cpl. G. Trigg of the
9th Battalion North Staffords, won
in the closing stages of the war.

North Staffords returned to Rawalpindi. Their task in the 1914-18 War would be a necessary but unglamorous one.

Besides the 1st, ten other battalions of the Regiment, apart from the 2nd in India, served overseas. The 4th was in France and Flanders in 1917-1918. The 1/5th and 1/6th T.F. were in the first territorial formation to go to France, in 1915, taking hard knocks at the Hohenzollern Redoubt at Loos, and at Gommecourt on the Somme. Their crowning glory, was an advance of 2,000 yards, capturing and crossing the bridge at Riqueval over the St. Quentin Canal, and breaking through defences as strong as any on the Western Front, in two and a half hours, one of the most brilliant performances by British infantry in the whole war.

The 2nd/5th and 2nd/6th T.F were unfortunate enough to be involved in the 1916 rebellion in Dublin. They then served on the Western Front, Lance-Cpl Thomas of the 2nd/5th earned the V.C at Cambrai in 1917.

The 7th Battalion fought at Gallipoli and later on in Mesopotamia, taking a distinguished part in the fighting around Kut-Al-Amara, and the advance to Baghdad. At Kut-Al-Amara Lt. Col. Henderson, wounded at Gallipoli, and since then commanding the 9th Royal Warwicks in the same brigade, earned a postumous V.C. The 7th Battalion now went to the Caucasus distinguishing itself defending Baku against the Bolshevists.

The 8th, 9th (Pioneer), 12th and 13th Battalions all served in France, the 8th doing especially well in the last German 1918 offensive at Mont de Bligny. Sergeant Carmichael of the 9th (Pioneer) Battalion earned his V.C. at Ypres in 1917.

This war record was one of which the Regiment, who in 1920 changed title to the North Staffordshire Regiment (The Prince of Wales's), could well be very proud. The Regiment was awarded 52 battle honours for the war, to add to their long list of honours; but it was ruled that only 10 of these were to be carried on the colours:

ARMENTIERES 1914, SOMME 1916, 18, ARRAS 1917,
MESSINES 1917,18, YPRES 1917,18, ST. QUENTIN CANAL,
SELLE, SARI BAIR, KUT AL AMARA 1917, N.W. FRONTIER INDIA 1915.

A 1914-18 khaki peaked cap with its original North Stafford cap badge.

46th
NORTH MIDLAND DIVISION.

BRITISH EXPEDITIONARY FORCE.

The Divisional Commander has received the following letter, dated 23rd November 1918, from General Sir. H. S. RAWLINSON, Bart., G.C.V.O., K.C.B., K.C.M.G., Commanding the Fourth Army, which he publishes with pride to all ranks of the Division :

" It is a matter of very deep regret to me that the 46th Division is not accompanying the Fourth Army to the Frontier. I desire, however, to place on record my appreciation of the splendid performances of the Division during the recent operations, and to congratulate all ranks on the conspicuous part they have played in the battles of the 100 days.

The forcing of the main Hindenburg line on the Canal, and the capture of *Bellenglise* ranks as one of the finest, and most dashing exploits of the war. The attacks of October 3rd, and the subsequent operations about *Bohain*, together with the later advance beyond the *Sambre* Canal, constitute a record of which all ranks of the Division may justly feel proud.

I offer to all ranks my warmest thanks for their great gallantry, and to the leaders and staffs my admiration of their skilful direction, and staff work throughout these battles.

To every Officer, N.C.O., and man of the Division I offer my warm thanks, and hearty congratulations, and trust that at some future time they may again form part of the Fourth Army. "

A letter from the 46th North Midland Divisional Commander, from General Sir H.S. Rawlinson, Bart., GCVO, KCB, KCMG, Commanding the Fourth Army, congratulating all ranks of the 46th Division on their gallantry, and the officers on their skillful direction and staff work throughout the recent battles

Twelve
The History of the 137th Staffordshire Brigade, 46th North Midland Division 1914-1918

Mobilisation for the Great War came on the 4th August 1914. The 46th North Midland Division Territorial Force came under Central Force (Home Defence), with HQs at the Hotel Metropole, London , where it was allocated to the Third Army commanded by Lt-General Sir W E Franklyn whose headquarters were in Luton, and where the Division was to be stationed.

Volunteers get their first taste of the Army in August 1914. 5th battalion, the Prince of Wales's, N. Staffs Regt.

The large expansion of the Territorial Force, and the raising of Kitchener's Army in 1914, over-taxed the resources causing considerable hardship to this vast number of men who had volunteered with such enthusiasm. In the early days of their training, instructors, uniforms, equipment and arms were all woefully short or non-existent and accommodation was either in billets or tents without floorboards. Broomsticks took the place of rifles and their unsuitable civilian clothing soon fell to pieces.

What instructors there were, were elderly and out of date. There was virtually no liaison between units at the Front and those at home. Many C.O.s were over the age limit or inefficient and had to be replaced before the unit went overseas. Those commanding reserves had neither knowledge nor the opportunity to teach their men modern warfare. Very often a man's first experience of battle training was when he went into action. In January 1915 the Territorial Force belatedly adopted the four-company system, but still retained its free-and-easy attitude to discipline and continued to wear the "T" on their officer's collar badges and the men's shoulder titles.

From the 4th August 1914, the influx of volunteers of all ages, for service with the colours, was overwhelming. As the war would "be over by Christmas" everyone wanted to get in on the action. Leek too had its volunteers seeking service with the 3rd Battery, although

A contemporary postcard of an unknown 46th North Midland Division Field Ambulance R.A.M.C. (TF) Sgt. Major, on the permanent staff c 1913.

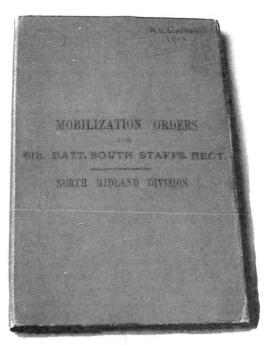

A set of Mobilisation Orders for the 6th South Staffs Regt., North Midland Division that were used in 1914.

it was already only about half a dozen short of the War Establishment, as were the other batteries in the 46th Brigade. Only the Brigade Ammunition Column was understrength, some of the men of the 3rd (Leek) Battery having been transferred to it. Unlike the Kitchener Volunteers, the Territorial Associations were able to clothe and equip the majority of their volunteers immediately.

The 46th (North Midland) Division consisted of the 137th (Staffordshire), 138th (Lincoln and Leicester) and the 139th (Sherwood Forester) Brigades. The 46th (North Midland) Division was the first complete Territorial Division to go to France in March 1915. Before going overseas the two Stafford battalions became the 1/5th and 1/6th. Whereas the regular units drew on their Depot and Special Reserve for reinforcements, the Territorial Force had to find their own reserves and these came from the 2/5th and 2/6th, and when these units also went on active service, from the 3/5th and 3/6th. The second line Territorial battalions from Staffordshire formed the 176th Brigade of the 59th Division, a duplicate of the 46th. Before going to France the 59th saw bitter fighting in the Dublin Rebellion of Easter 1916. The Division remained in Ireland until 1917 and then went to France, via Salisbury Plain.

Following brief 'trench instruction', April 1915 saw the 46th (North Midland) Division march from Ballieul into Belgium, taking over the 28th Division's trenches between Kemmel and Wulverghem. Brigadier-General E. Feetham, the former Commanding Officer of the 2nd Battalion, the Royal Berkshire Regiment, took over command just prior to the Staffordshire Brigade going into the line.

After heavy fighting in 1914, the Germans had captured Messines Ridge. The British position now dug into a small ridge in front of Wulverghem. The North Midland Division was initiated into trench warfare here, considered a relatively quiet sector. The 137th Staffordshire

Brigade of the North Midland Division was responsible for the southern part, a frontage of about 2,000 yards. Two main roads divided the Brigade's line, in the centre, the road from Wytschaete to Wulverghem, and to the south, the road from Messines to Wulverghem which doubled as the Divisional boundary. The Brigade's battalions moved to their billets near Neuve Eglise, on 2nd April. The South Staffordshire battalions went to Bulford Camp, the North Stafford's to Aldershot Camp. The 1/5th South Staffs and 1/5th North Staffs marched from Neuve Eglise to take over the line later that evening. Initially the weather was bad, the battalions being rotated after a few days. On the evening of 5th April, the 1/6th North Staffs relieved the 1/5th North Staffs. The 1/5th South Staffs waited until the next evening to be relieved by 1/6th South Staffs. In daylight there was sniper and artillery fire, so the reliefs were carried out at night if possible.

During their time at Wulverghem, the North and South Staffs alternated with each other, a tour in the front line usually lasting four days. It is interesting that the 6-gun 18 pdr batteries of the regulars were replaced by the 4-gun 15pdr BLCs of the Territorials, a reduction of strength on this front meaning less support for the infantry.

A contemporary postcard of the "C" (3rd Leek, Staffs.) Battery, 231st Brigade RFA 46th North Midland Division TF - armed with an obsolescent 15 pdr BLC prior to the start of the Great War.

When the Staffords took over, the trenches comprised of a single line of unconnected breastworks and ditches, with no second-line or communication trenches. Relief units crossed open ground to reach the front line. Contemporary accounts state there was a pungent smell of rotting vegetation in the front line trenches. The rudimentary trenches required work parties to maintain and try to improve them, including barbed wire in front. This work was often carried out at night under fire.

The area was dotted with farms, those closest to the front line reinforced by the construction of redoubts called Strong Points (SPs), accommodating a platoon and machine

An original photograph of Friday 14th August 1914, of the "C" (3rd Leek, Staffs.) Battery, 231st Brigade RFA column at the bottom of Derby Street and Ashbourne Road in Leek on their way to rendezvous with the 46th North Midland Division TF who were concentrating in the Luton area.

gun post. SP4, at North Midland Farm, was garrisoned by the South Staffs; SP5, later known as Fort Pinkie, was garrisoned by the North Staffs. Burnt Farm and Monmouth Farm formed the second-line defence in the Staffordshire Brigades' sector. The North Staffs HQ was at R.E. Farm. The South Staffs HQ was at Wulverghem Cabaret, whose kitchen was the phone exchange. Souvenir Farm was used for trench stores.

The Staffs units had a steady stream of casualties from sniping and shelling. Regimental Aid Posts (RAPs) dealt with these close to the front line, at R.E. Farm for the North Staffs and St. Quentin Cabaret, an inn, for the South Staffs. R.E. Farm had been a dressing station in the earlier fighting. Those killed were buried close by in the cemetery at R.E. Farm or Wulverghem churchyard. Not all wounds were from enemy action. The War Diary of the 1/6th North Staffs records that between 16th-20th May, the Battalion had two killed and three wounded. The injured men had self-inflicted wounds.

Snipers were a constant threat in the trenches. Initially the units of the Brigade were woefully ill-equipped to snipe from their own trenches, without specialist rifles or telescopic sights. Captain W. Millner of the 1/5th South Staffs narrowly avoided being killed while sniping on 5th May. One of the best shots in the country at the time, Millner was an ideal candidate. While observing German movements from the barn of one of the farms close to the front line, he was wounded by an enemy sniper. The bullet hit the cap badge of his cap and creased his skull. His injury was not serious and after a brief spell he returned to the front. On the other hand, on the 20th July, 'C' (3rd Leek, Staffs) Battery, 231st Brigade RFA, 46th Division received their first fatality in the same way. Lieut Basil Nicholson had just returned from leave at his home, Highfield Hall, Leek, when he heard his brother, Capt. Falkner

Nicholson had earlier in the day been wounded in the shoulder by shrapnel.

Gnr Lorenzo Pickford, shortly to be severely wounded in the leg, described the incident. *"Basil made it clear he intended to retaliate for his brother's misfortune. Along with Frank Bowcock the signaller, they made their way to the front line trench and the Observation Post (OP). Basil relayed the order to the four guns to fire a simultaneous salvo. He then looked out from the OP to ascertain the result, when, unknown to the unfortunate Basil, a German sniper was waiting for just such a moment. It was all over in seconds, the sniper fired one round, and shot Basil in the head, killing him instantly".*

The Battery and the people of Leek were stunned by the news of the death. The burial took place the following day and Driver Bert "Dingle" Sheldon collected Capt. Falkner Nicholson from hospital to attend his brother's funeral at the small churchyard in Dranoutre.

A picture of Lieut Basil Lee Nicholson who was the Leek Battery's first loss, 24th July 1915 from *Leek and District Sailors & Soldiers Roll of Honour 1914-1915* published by David Morris & Co, Printers, Leek

Whilst a battery was in the line, an officer of the battery always had to be FOO (Forward Observation Officer), but this was shared amongst the subalterns and their batmen. Communication telephone lines between the FOO and the guns had to be installed and manned by the signallers, in the case of the 'C' (3rd Leek, Staffs) Battery, by Frank Bowcock, Corporals Harry Bailey, H Crabtree and J Phillips. The installation and manning of these was particularly dangerous with the resultant highest casualty rate. Shell fire constantly damaged the lines necessitating continual repairs. This is well illustrated by the four Leek Battery telephonists. Frank Bowcock received the DCM, Harry Bailey received the MM, and was later killed, Harry Crabtree and J Phillips were also both killed in action.

The Messines Ridge gave a good view, and the enemy regularly shelled the British lines. Such bombardments could be devastating. On the 6th May Trench 8, positioned astride the Wulverghem-Messines Road, was heavily shelled, wounding nine men. Despite his wounds, Sgt. Pitt reorganised the South Staffs garrison and was commended for his bravery.

There were friendly fire caused casualties too. On 29th April, 10B Trench, held by 'A' Company of the 1/5th South Staffs, was hit by a 'short' from a British battery. Pte B. Martin of the Machine Gun Section was killed when his dug-out collapsed and three others were wounded by the shrapnel.

Mining had started before the Staffords arrived. The 172nd Tunnelling Company of the Royal Engineers was in action near Kruisstraat Cabaret, in front of the North and South Staffs close to Boyles Farm. The sappers were short handed, so the Staffs formed a Brigade Mining Section. Many of the men had been miners in peacetime so recruits were easy to get.

The Brigade Mining Section was only involved in defensive mining, counter-mining and exploding charges, called camoflets, under the German tunnels. On 27th April during such an operation, carbon-monoxide fumes overcame some men from the Mining Section who needed rescuing. The DCM Medal was awarded to nine members of the rescue party, all the men receiving the same citation. Six of those decorated came from the Staffordshire Brigade Mining Section. The award of the medals, the first to the Staffs Brigade, was a source of great pride.

On 22nd April the enemy used gas, far to the north of the sector. Rudimentary anti-gas pads were issued. On the evening of 8th May, there was a gas alert in the North Midland Division's sector, later discovered to be the odour of a decomposing cow - but, to the men that evening, the threat was real enough.

Late in May, the Staffords spent two weeks, in training units of the 14th (Light) Division, in trench warfare. Despite some action, life was tedious now. Daily routine began and ended with "Stand-to", troops fixing bayonets for any German dawn or dusk attack. The rest of the day was spent digging and repairing the trenches, eating, trying to sleep or dealing with body lice, the bane of a soldier's life. After a tour of duty in the front line, the battalions would march back to Neuve Eglise for a period of rest - the term being misleading. The billets, Aldershot and Bulford Camps, were newly erected huts with windows on one side, that faced the German lines, blocked up. Straw was laid on the floor for bedding, whilst light was supplied by a single oil lamp. Located in the camps were the RE Stores, providing tools for the working parties. The infantry, under the supervision of sappers from 1/2nd North Midland Field Company, often provided these working

parties. Such work, during a period of 'rest', was disliked. The situation was made worse as the men of the Royal Engineers enjoyed higher pay. When not on work parties, rest meant a daily round of inspections, route marches and other duties.

However, there was some relaxation. Sports, particularly football, had always been encouraged by the Army to foster unit pride and maintain moral. Therefore, inter-unit football matches were organised, along with concerts, religious services and the traditional Church Parade. Bath facilities were created near the rest camps. In Kemmel, the vats of a local brewery were converted into a bathhouse. Others were made of tarpaulins in nearby farms. Soldier's clothing was boiled destroying the lice eggs, allowing the men a short respite. Rest periods also allowed the men to write home, some letters being published to satisfy the desire for news in Staffordshire. All letters were subject to censorship, place names and movements being omitted or erased.

The end of June saw the 46th Division ordered north into the Ypres Salient. 137th Brigade was relieved by the 149th (Northumberland Fusiliers Brigade of 50th, Northumbrian, Division). The Staffs Brigade marched to their new billets at Ouderdom on 25th June, leaving some of their comrades as silent sentinels in the local cemeteries. When not in the line near Hill 60, the 46th

*The 137th Staffordshire Brigade
at the capture of St Quentin Canal, 1918.
(Rob Chapman, Flintlock Publishing).*

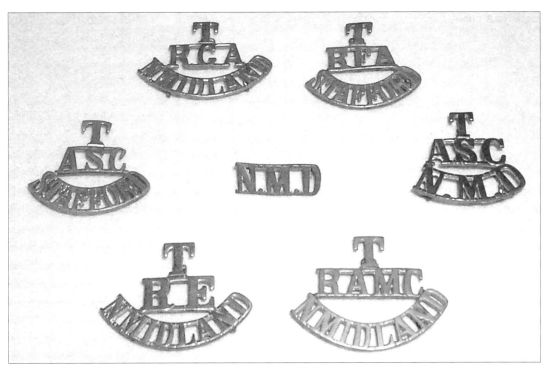

An incomplete collection of 1914-1918 War brass shoulder titles of the corps attached to the 46th N. Midland Division including A.S.C., R.A.M.C., R.G.A., R.E.

The original uniform of Captain F.E. Taylor of the 1/5th North Staffs Regt., with his territorial "T" still below his collar dogs

Division was in support or reserve near Dickebusch. How the troops spent their time either in the trenches or out maybe judged from this extract from the 6th Battalion South Staffs history:

> *'If all the troops with all the tools*
> *Should dig for half a year,*
> *'Do you suppose,' the Colonel asked,*
> *'That we should then be clear?'*
> *'I doubt it,' said the Adjutant*
> *'Knowing the Brigadier.'*

Before taking part in its first real battle, the North Midland Division had a wide experience of trench life in some of the Western Front's grimmest and most dangerous sections. At the beginning of October the 46th (North Midland) Division moved south from the Ypres Salient to take its part in the battle of Loos. During a reconnaissance, Waterhouse, CO of the 1/6th South Staffs, was severely wounded and although he had an excellent successor in Colonel Law, his loss was unfortunate. In the later phase of Loos, the 46th Division was to attack the Hohenzollern redoubt and Fosse 8, over much the same ground as the 1st Battalion of the South Staffs had also tried, and failed. Full of confidence and anxious to distinguish itself, the North Midland Division was given an impossible task on that fine, sunny afternoon of the 13th October.

The 231st Brigade RFA from reserve, of which 'C' (3rd Leek, Staffs) Battery were part, was ordered to shell the Hohenzollern Redoubt in support of the 5th and 6th North Staffs. At the time, the Leek lads did not know they were witnessing a black day in the history of North Staffordshire. Even at this late date, the British bombardments still had negligible effect on the strong enemy defences. A hail of machine-gun fire on the assembly trenches was a warning of the ordeal to follow. It can be imagined with what reluctance COs warned brigades of the futility of any advance under such conditions, yet the suicidal attempt was made. It is a pity those giving the orders were not in the trenches to lead the troops, for, if they had survived they would never give such orders again!

As it was at 2pm the long lines of infantry advanced in daylight, making perfect targets for the efficient and deadly machine guns, who mowed down the Staffords.   The attack was a blind assault across 'no mans land', the majority of the attacking North Staffords being shot dead within ten minutes, most on their own parapet, and it was with sadly depleted ranks that the first objective was reached. Now any further progress could only be made there by bombing and in this connection the 1/5th South Staffs War Diary reports that the lighter enemy grenades far outranged the Mills. However, with more practice the range of the grenade was increased. As bombers got more used to the Mills grenade, it became and remained the most efficient grenade in use, its main disadvantage then being its weight.

At about noon on the 14th, the forward troops were ordered to retire back to their original front line. The flower of Staffordshire's territorials were dead. The two South Staffs Battalions had lost 31 officers and 695 other ranks killed, wounded or missing (many, of course, dead). The two North Staffs Battalions had lost 37 officers and 783 other ranks killed, wounded or missing. The system of continuing attacks after repeated failures was futile and hideously wasteful and you cannot avoid the conclusion that the whole tragedy of Loos was largely the fault of the senior commanders and their staffs.

A postcard of the 5th or 6th North Staffs. The usual bravado/enthusiasm of men going to the front is plainly absent in these battle weary troops, who are obviously out of the line. I strongly believe, from what is written on the reverse of this postcard, that this is a handful of the survivors of the battle of Loos.

After the evacuation of Gallipoli, the British Government was disturbed by Turkish forecasts of the recapture of Egypt, which would close the Suez Canal. Ignoring the fact that the attack would require planning and organisation beyond the Turks, if it was to succeed, the garrison in Egypt was strengthened by moving troops, who could be ill-spared, from France. After Loos the 46th (North Midland) Division received large reinforcements, before taking over trenches from an Indian Division at Neuve Chapelle. The former occupants were probably Gurkhas as the trenches were only three feet deep. They were also waterlogged, as November 1915 was very wet, but apart from the discomfort and digging required, things were quiet.

On the 12th November whilst in the Armentieres Sector, the Brigade finally got rid of their old 15 pdrs that were by now very worn and inaccurate. At Lestrem Railway Station they were replaced with brand new 18 pdr QF. The battery establishment still remained at four guns. On relief early in December, the Division was surprised to receive lectures on "Duties on board ship" - which gave them something else to think about other than the non-stop rain! There were also courses in open warfare well behind the line, another move indication. On Christmas Day the 137th Brigade entrained for Marseilles and the men realised for the first time that France did not entirely consist of muddy trenches and uncomfortable rest camps and billets. Marseilles even in winter provided sunshine and sea-bathing - it was with regret that the Staffords embarked on board ship.

At first it was assumed that Gallipoli was the destination, but when the evacuation took place, it was learnt that the Division was en route for the Suez Canal. The 1/5th and 1/6th South Staffs embarked in *H.M.S. Magnificent* on 2nd January 1916. As this elderly battleship also carried two RE Field Companies, accommodation must have been nicely crowded. The North Staffs embarked on the P & O Liner, *Beltana*, the men finding the quarters on this vessel most comfortable. The men were given hammocks to sleep in, and had to put them up themselves. This caused considerable amusement - *"Chaps were swinging all ways, and getting tipped out"* (Pte. Sherratt). The *Beltana* arrived in Alexandria on the 12th, and the North Staffs were immediately taken by train to the north side of the Suez Canal, to Shalufa. The two South Staffs units also disembarked at Alexandria, going by train to Shalufa.

Law, the CO of the 1/6th South Staffs, crossed the canal to contact the Indian regiment which was to be relieved. This was simple, for the Indian unit handed over one machine gun and a coil of rusty barbed wire and departed. Much to their surprise the Staffords were not required to dig and after they had spent a short while training in the desert, they were soon back in Alexandria and embarked in a troop ship for a comfortable return journey to Marseilles. The futility of the move was proved a few months later when the Turks made a half-hearted attack on the Canal, to be beaten off with great ease; a few pontoons littered the east bank for many years. To add to the absurdity of the whole affair, the Staffordshire Regiments were awarded the battle honour, EGYPT, 1916.

Returning from Egypt, the 46th (North Midland) Division took over a sector from the French, at Neuville, North of Arras. These trenches had only been recently captured from the Germans, who were determined to retake them, and were making much use of mining. These enemy mines had only one advantage for the happy-go-lucky, thriftless soldier - any piece of missing kit was always "blowed up" by a mine and had to be replaced by a reluctant and suspicious quartermaster. One soldier of the 1/6th South Staffs was truly "blowed up" and came down in the enemy trenches to survive as a prisoner-of-war. What would appear to be unnecessary risks were taken by our 'Heavies', whose 9.2 shells all too often fell short - the 1/5th South Staffs had several casualties in this manner. They also did great damage to the trenches. In some places the two lines were only some twenty yards apart, and the resentful infantry considered these ponderous weapons might have been more usefully and safely employed on more distant targets.

In May the Division was in the line between Arras and Albert, at Fondquevilliers, and here the two South Staffs Battalions were much amused when the enemy opposite vacated their trenches during a false alarm and then methodically bombed their way back to find nobody there! On the 13th May the 2nd North Midland Brigade, RFA, now became the 231st Brigade RFA with Batteries A, B, C and D. The 3rd (Leek) Battery now became 'C' Battery. On the 26th May further artillery re-organisation followed. 'D' Battery's 18 pdrs were replaced by 4.5" Howitzers. Territorial RFA Brigades (on a lower establishment than regulars) now were mixed with 4-4.5" Howitzers and 12-18 pdrs. The Howitzer Brigades were disbanded. From now on all artillery brigades in the RFA were mixed. Throughout May and June, when out of the trenches, working parties were continuous and arduous, when the troops should really have been training for the ordeal ahead.

On 14th June 1916, Rettemoy Farm, a well-known enemy strongpoint, was shelled by 'C' (Leek) Battery. This, along with Bois Biez, was to be a pain in the neck to the 5th North Staffs on the 46th North Midland Brigade's return visit in March 1917. On 17th June the 231st Brigade RFA HQ moved to Gaudiempre, as the batteries in the Haie valley had been constantly observed by German balloons in Logeast WD, and were attracting counter-battery fire, despite the Royal Flying Corps best efforts. On the 23rd-24th June, the 231st Brigade RFA targeted Gommecourt in preparation for the Somme offensive, concentrating on attempted wire cutting, registration, destruction of defences etc by day, and harassing fire at

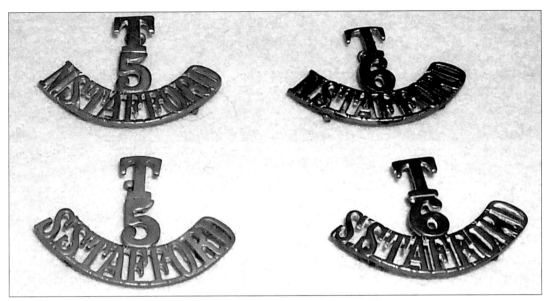

A complete collection of T/5 and T/6 North and South Staffs brass shoulder titles, of the 1914-1918 War

night. Over 10,000 rounds were fired in the seven days prior to the infantry assault (the average life of an 18pdr field gun was 20,000 rounds firing on full charge). At a 'stand easy', cold water poured into the muzzles was scalding hot when it ran out of the breaches, and as a result of the heat, the mineral jelly lubricant in the gun recuperators was losing its viscosity so quickly, it ran out, causing constant seizures.

Neither the place nor the time of the British offensive in the summer of 1916 were favoured by General Haig, who would have preferred to attack further north in Flanders and after his reinforcements had received more battle training. By this time, the main burden of defeating the Germans was beginning to be borne by Britain, and the French, hard pressed at Verdun, urgently requested speedy action so that the Allies could attack side by side. The Somme area was chosen. The ground had not been fought over before and the British hoped they would be free of the appalling mud and shell holes of Flanders. Considering this, it was indeed unfortunate that the very wet weather in May and June, and the strong German counter measures, turned the area into a vast morass, greatly hindering the assembly of troops and the moving up of the many guns, with their enormous stocks of shells.

The British were to attack to the north of the Somme, on a line stretching from Gommecourt, a few miles south of Arras, to Curlu on the Somme, whilst the French attacked simultaneously to the south. The British aim, in the opening stage of the battle, was the German first line. To make the attack effective it was decided to at first destroy the enemy's lines by a prolonged bombardment. To do this on so large a front involved an enormous amount of artillery fire - now possible because of the increased munitions production.

Preparations were elaborate, and took considerable time. Vast amounts of ammunition and stores of all sorts needed to be accumulated close to the front. Railways and tramways were built and roads improved. Dugouts were provided for the troops, and as magazines and dressing stations. Miles of deep communication trenches were dug, as well as advance trenches, for the day of the attack. Much of this was done under fire. The weather was bad and the local accommodation totally inadequate to house the troops who had to content themselves with such rough shelter as could be provided. All this labour was carried out in addition to the everyday fighting and maintenance of existing defences.

The German position was formidable, situated on high undulating ground, rising about 500 feet above sea level. Having held the positions for two years, the Germans had spared no effort to render them impregnable. The first and second systems each consisted of several lines of deep trenches, well provided with bomb-proof shelters, and numerous communication trenches connecting them. The front of the trenches in each system was protected by wire entanglements, many of them in two belts forty yards broad, built of iron stakes interlaced with barbed wire, almost as thick as a man's finger. In addition the villages and woods were made into fortresses, and machine-gun redoubts had been built to protect important points. Behind all this were heavy masses of artillery, who knew to a foot the range of their own and the British trenches.

It was against such positions that the 46th (North Midland) Division were to make their attack, and they were put on the extreme north against one of the most formidable points, Gommecourt. The British High Command hoped that, with the greatest preliminary bombardment ever known, followed by very powerful infantry attacks, the German lines would be pierced, the enemy would lose their good observation posts and open warfare would develop - for as yet the immense strength of the enemy defences was not

realised. The artillery concentrations started on 24th June with the 18-pounders firing at the German wire and were joined by the howitzers and mediums on the 26th. According to the History of the 2nd Division, the British fired well over a million shells between 24th June and 1st July. Owing to the heavy and persistent rain and the disappointing results of the wire-cutting, the initial infantry attacks were postponed from 29th June to 1st July.

The enemy had anticipated the chief British thrust would be in the Gommecourt area and consequently were fully prepared. An assembly line was quickly and skilfully dug by the 137th Brigade, but the artillery bombardment before

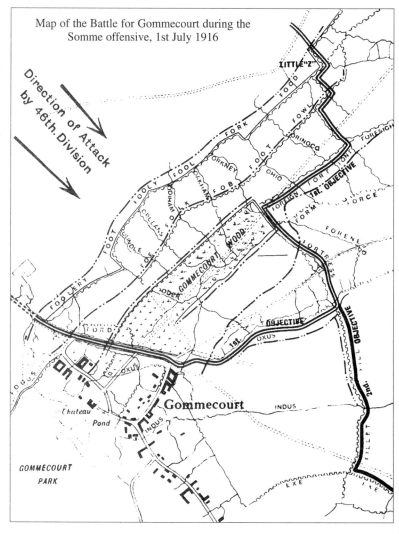

Map of the Battle for Gommecourt during the Somme offensive, 1st July 1916

the attack prevented any possibility of surprise. The sharp and accurate reply on the British working parties before the actual attack left no illusions on the efficiency of the German gunners.

On 1st July at 7.30am the British barrage lifted and the 137th Staffordshire Brigade went over the top with the 1/6th North Staffs on the left and the 1/6th South Staffs on the right, each followed by their own 1/5ths. There were four waves at eighty yards distance, the whole of the 137th Brigade was committed. 'C' (Leek) Battery covered the assault of the 139th Infantry Brigade 5th and 7th Sherwood Foresters. To assist the barrage, smoke was used, but unsuccessfully as it drifted parallel to the trenches and not towards the enemy, so that half way across 'no man's land' the attackers came into full view of the Germans. Even initially when the smoke was effective the enemy machine guns firing on fixed lines mowed down the British. As normal, the wire-cutting by the guns was ineffective; though a company of the 1/6th South Staffs found one gap, some men actually reached the enemy front line, only to be overwhelmed and killed. Elsewhere, according to Captain Mander, who made an inspection under fire and was lucky to survive, there were no further gaps. The artillery available was simply insufficient with catastrophic results for the infantry.

Throughout the attacks, a series of enemy barrages on 'no man's land' and our forward and communication trenches, caused numerous casualties. The R.A.M.C. also got a full share of these. On the left the Sherwood Forester Brigade were also getting annihilated, and by noon the remnants of the attackers were forced to withdraw, and a further contemplated attack was wisely aborted. Though the Gommecourt offensive had forced the enemy to deploy guns and troops urgently to the north, the dreadful carnage was unjustifiable. The 46th (North Midland) Division suffered appallingly. Quoting Lieut. Walter Meakin of the 5th North Staffs:

"Our attack at Gommecourt was as heroic as anything in the War.... Through the enemy's three barrages of intense fire our men marched quite steadily, as if nothing was in the way, as if they were under review. At every step men fell..... When these steady, steadfast soldiers, true to the death, paraded in more than decimated numbers through and across the third barrage, the enemy-in their turn heroic-left their trenches, erected machine-guns on the parapets, and the two parties fought one another in the open. I have not the hardihood to write more....Heroism could no further go. Our men died; and in dying held in front of them enough German guns to alter the fate of our principal and our most successful advance in the South. They died defeated, but won as great a victory in spirit and in fact as English history or any history will ever chronicle".

Reinforcements were not available, being sent to units still engaged in the offensive. The depleted 46th (North Midland) Division was ordered to a quiet portion of the line three miles north of Gommecourt, with the 137th Staffordshire Brigade at Berles-au-Bois, or close behind. The frontage here was so extended that only listening posts could be manned. Luckily the Germans did not take advantage of this weakness, confining their activities to occasional shelling. The total British casualties for the Somme offensive are estimated at 450,000 and the results on the whole were disappointing with no break-through and in some sectors little if any gain of ground to offset the enormous loss. To the south, divisional commanders were not allowed to exploit any successes, and along the front the incoordination between the infantry and artillery was painfully obvious. The gallantry of our infantry could not conceal the poor training of the drafts that formed a large proportion of the battalions, and the standard of musketry had dropped.

Gradually reinforcements arrived and amongst these were thirteen officers commissioned from Scottish units and posted to the 1/6th South Staffs. After courses at which according to the C.O. *"they instructed the instructors",* they rendered yeoman service. On 5th August, aircraft for the first time registered enemy targets for the 231st Brigade RFA, via the new Mark V Tuner, a wireless set giving ground-air communications. The 29th August saw the Brigade officially increased to six gun batteries, though the extra guns had been received prior to the re-organisation. With the increase in establishment, and replacements, the local character of the 231st Brigade RFA batteries was diluted.

A silver hip flask engraved 2nd Lieut. H. Swindells, 1/5th South Staffs (killed in action on 15th August 1917)

Successful raids early in September killed Germans, brought in prisoners and many useful documents. This received praise, which was welcome to the depressed troops following the Somme, from which so much had been hoped. Further raids in October brought more prisoners, but no papers, as apparently security measures had been tightened by the enemy. In November, Brigadier-General Campbell VC took over the 137th Staffordshire Brigade. To give an idea of trench conditions during the winter, one Lewis-gun post near Monchy was actually on an island.

Other hardships, besides the German shelling and the appalling weather, as far as the officers were concerned, included ever increasing paperwork. A trench log book had to include every event of the day, details of stores handed, or taken, over etc. Additionally no less than twelve other daily returns were required, commencing with a morning situation return due at about 3.30am and finishing late at night with a frostbite treatment certificate. When a French unit relieved a British one, the French adjutant or equivalent arrived with all his documents in an attaché case; his British counterpart needed a limber. Sympathy can be felt for an overworked adjutant, who when asked why duck-boards were needed, wrote back *"Owing to the War!"*

There was some anxiety about the performance of the 18pdr. Early in 1917 orders were given that an 18pdr should never exceed a firing rate of 4 rounds per minute as they would not stand more. Higher rates of fire were causing "gun wear" in the barrels. A cause for concern for the remainder of the war.

March 1917 saw the Germans start their retreat, with them increasing the shelling around Monchy, and the 46th Division patrols being sharply engaged. The Germans had withdrawn to Bucquoy, three miles east of disastrous Gommecourt, by the 9th, and the 137th Staffordshire Brigade was ordered to attack this village, as it was thought to be lightly held. From the outset the attack was a fiasco, orders being changed at the last moment. The 1/6th South Staffs only received their orders six hours before the attack was to start - consequently not taking part at all.

All the North Staffords that had died on the previous 1st July still lay out in no-man's land in heaps, just as they had fallen. Looking through binoculars, it could be seen the enemy's wire was still eerily covered with the bodies of the men of the North Staffs.

The actual attack was to be made by the North and South Staffs 1/5ths, the South Staffs to the right, and zero was at 1.00am on 14th March. At 6pm the previous evening the 1/5th South Staffs were at Souastre, five miles from their start point at Biez Wood, a mile west of Bucquoy. En route they were delayed, probably at Fonquevilliers, by troops and transport awaiting the cessation of the gas shelling of the village. The Battalion reached its assembly position less than an hour before zero, having had a tiring march, heavily laden, over thick mud - just before being expected to make an attack across unknown territory in darkness without time to re-organise themselves, or even to get a heartening cup of tea.

Despite all this the troops advanced gallantly until reaching the enemy wire, when as usual the fallacy that barrages, however accurate, could cut, let alone destroy, well-laid wire, was disproved in the usual tragic manner. Any gaps caused bunching, with the German machine guns decimating the Staffords in the light of flares. A few of the 1/5th Staffords got a foothold in the enemy trenches, but without reinforcements were driven out by strong counter-attacks. The failure was attributable to the uncut wire, disorganisation due to early and severe officer and NCO casualties, darkness and ignorance of the ground, lack of grenades and difficulties in communications. Another important factor was the unexpectedly strong resistance, but also the shocking staff work before the attack, that rendered it hopeless from the outset.

Both the North and South Staffs were rightly praised for their gallant attempt. The 1/6th reached Biez Wood and was not in action until the 18th when they pursued the retiring enemy, until squeezed out of the fray by converging British divisions on its left and right flank and rejoining the Brigade in salvage work.

In April and May 1917 the 46th (North Midland) Division was in the Lieven-Angres sector, south-west of Lens, still held by the Germans. There was fierce fighting north of Lens on the 24th and 25th May when an attack by the North Staffs supported by the 1/6th South Staffs was repulsed. Trench life was made very hazardous by enemy mortars firing 'pineapples' until the arrival of the Stokes Mortar, when retaliatory measures could take place. On the 9th June No. 2 gun of 'C' (Leek) Battery received a direct hit, killing Sgt G Bestwick, a former Rifle Volunteer and two gunners, who were buried in the military section of Fosse Dix cemetery.

The beginning of June saw the 137th Staffordshire Brigade in the Loos-Lens area making large raids in which the two participating companies were well supported by divisional artillery. These were preparatory for the full scale attack on Lens on the 28th. The 46th Division had three brigades forward, with the 137th Staffordshire Brigade to the centre, the Foresters on the left, and the Leicester and Lincoln to the right. The Stafford's objectives were the Cite de Moulin on the town's western edge, and the nearby 'Aconite Trench'. The 1/6th North Staffs were on the left and the 1/5th South Staffs on the right, with the 1/6th South Staffs finding one company in close support, two as carrying parties and the other improving communications. Zero was at 7.10pm. A thunderstorm did little to help.

Both South Staffs COs state in their reports that the men moved too close behind their barrage, an excellent tribute to the artillery. Due to the artillery, German resistance on the right was under expectation, with light casualties initially. The 1/5th South Staffs consolidated their objective during the night. The North Staffs however experienced stronger resistance and along with a 1/6th South Staffs platoon were forced back with most men killed or wounded. The attack resumed on the 30th and after desperate fighting the trenches were re-captured. An attempt to advance into Lens by the 1/5th North Staffs, supported by the 1/6th South Staffs against well barricaded and little-damaged houses, full of machine guns, was a costly failure. Owing to the closeness of the houses no artillery support was possible.

The 137th Staffordshire Brigade was relieved on the 1st July with many gaps in its ranks. The 46th Division Artillery 230th and 231st Brigades RFA also suffered very severe casualties during July 1917, these casualties, in the main, from the constant heavy enemy shell fire, that out-ranged the British guns.

The summer of 1917 saw the enemy building many concrete machine-gun emplacements known as 'pill-boxes'. These were normally half buried and they were proof against anything except a direct hit from a heavy gun. Being well camouflaged they were difficult to locate and were most formidable defences. After the battle of Lens, the 46th (North Midland) Division went to a rest and training centre for about three weeks, returning to take over trenches between Hulluch and Loos in late July. The enemy here were reported as nervous and content to remain on the defensive, as confirmed by successful patrols and raids by the Staffords. One German prisoner had a grudge against his company commander, pointing out his dug-out on a trench map. British guns duly registered on it.

There was considerable rivalry between the 1/5th and 1/6th on taking prisoners during raids. To make things worse, when the 5th South Staffs had made several ineffective attempts, a German walked across to surrender - to the 6th! The enemy held their front line very lightly and at night left only a few listening posts. Whilst the German High Command had no hesitation in demanding great sacrifices from the troops on occasions, it must be admitted its man management was far superior to that of the Allies.

The 137th Staffordshire Brigade remained in the same sector until the end of 1917, in the trenches south-west of Hulluch, or in so-called rest billets at various mining villages near Bethune. In the latter, the men were much better off than the muddy camps. The War Diaries of both South Staffs units give tribute to administrative arrangements behind the lines. Health was good except for the odd case of venereal disease, games and concerts are often mentioned, and leave parties left regularly and swiftly for home. Following the enemy's practice, since the introduction of tanks, each battery now positioned one gun as far forward as possible in an anti-tank role, as the enemy was expected to use captured British Mk. IV tanks.

When the 1/6th South Staffs stood to on Christmas morning the men were politely greeted with *"Happy Christmas"* by the enemy opposite!

The 137th Staffordshire Brigade started 1918 in the Hulluch sector and a change was made in leading patrols, formerly considered to be the task of a junior officer. When NCOs took turns with the subalterns they soon gained the necessary experience and did equally good work. British raids on German trenches all across the front were now identifying many enemy divisions from the Eastern Front, and there was unhappy speculation as to when and where to expect an enemy attack. Frost and snow followed by thaws damaged the trenches. One company of the 1/5th South Staffs applied for trench pumps. Towards the end of January companies were reduced from four to three platoons and, with the introduction of the three-battalion brigade, the 137th Staffordshires lost the 1/5th North Staffs with great regret.

Training was interrupted by intensive wiring both in front and behind the lines, that at

Military Medal & 1914 - 15 Star Trio

Cpl. 820466 A. H. Watson - 46th North Midland Division.

Ammunition Column. Royal Field Artillery. Territoral Force.

Army Form W/ 3121 - Reccommendation's For Honour / Reward

June 21st 1917

"2 men, one of whom: L/Cpl Watson showed great courage, and devotion, and resourse, during an enemy raid on positions. On previous occasion's he has shown the greatest disregard for danger".

The Military Medal and and 1914/15 Trio of Cpl. A.H. Watson,
46th North Midland Division, Ammunition Column

World War 1 postcard of Lewis gunners of the 1/5th South Staffs

the time was criticised as a waste of time. But, this would prove to be a wise precaution in time to come, especially with the alarming reports coming in of substantial enemy reinforcements from the Russian Front.

Following a month in billets, the 46th (North Midland) Division returned to the line, the 1/5th taking over some mine buildings, formerly occupied by enemy prisoners, that according to rumour were moved after bombs had been dropped nearby. By the 5th March the 137th Staffordshire Brigade were in brickworks in the Cuinchy sector south of La Bassee Canal; the tunnels and bricks of which prevented many casualties from the intensifying enemy bombardments. Reports from prisoners and a strong and successful enemy raid on a neighbouring brigade all indicated the great German offensive was not far off. Units of the Division were well up to strength and their morale was high.

Three days later, on 21st March, the enemy broke through south of Arras. The 46th (North Midland) Division was told the enemy opposite had been strongly reinforced and that an attack was imminent. If so, it may have been postponed by our accurate shelling of enemy communications. On the 27th the Division was ordered to relieve a Canadian division at Lens, the latter being required further south where the situation was desperate. The 46th (North Midland) Division bitterly resented the implication that they were second rate to the Canadians and indeed there was a good deal of indignation among English units, that formed by far the vast bulk of the Expeditionary Force, that so much prominence was given by the British Press to Colonials and Highlanders and so little to their own share of the fighting. However by the 28th the relief was safely accomplished under difficult circumstances.

18957/20017/203311 Private John Allen
1/5th Battalion South Staffordshire Regiment
Killed in Action 14th March 1917

The casualty trio (without death plaque) of Pte. J. Allen of the 1/5th South Staffs,
who was killed in action on 14th March 1917

There were many gas shells at Lens and a vicious air attack on the transport lines of the 1/6th South Staffs, but no infantry assault and the Division was relieved on 11th April. It took over the line north of La Bassee Canal on the 25th, a long sector with the shallow trenches occupied by two battalions, covering Bethune, and with approaches fully exposed to enemy fire. The 1/5th South Staffs had an engagement on the 26th when a platoon strong-point was heavily shelled and then rushed. It took two counter-attacks, involving two companies, to regain the captured position, with a loss of eight officers and over 100 other ranks. But many enemy troops were killed, 54 prisoners taken and three machine guns captured. The Battalion was deservedly congratulated on its tenacity and courage.

There was considerable gas shelling in early May and on the 21st the 137th Staffordshire Brigade suffered one of the worst gas bombardments of the entire war. An area of 10,000 square yards was hit by an enormous number of shells, the Brigade suffering the brunt of this dense concentration. The Staffords were terribly affected, the 1/6th South Staffs alone having well over 300 gas casualties, not only from the actual shelling, but also the deadly vapour that the sun released next day. Some died in hospital, many suffered the after-effects for life. So desperate was the need for men that the Staffords could only be relieved for four days. On their return the 1st Monmouths helped out the weaker units. Both Staffordshire Territorial Brigades received heavy losses from enemy mustard gas.

During the summer of 1918 the situation for the Allies brightened considerably. A steady trickle of reinforcements from other fronts reached the British Army and, though these troops had little knowledge of trench warfare, they were otherwise well trained. The French Army had much improved and the continuous arrival of Americans inspired their war worn predecessors with fresh conviction. On the other side, things were going badly for the Germans; their civilians were complaining bitterly about the lack of food. Though most of the enemy army fought on, certain formations, according to Ludendorf, had lost their enthusiasm. The German navy, bottled up in port, were disorderly and discontent, and Germany's unreliable allies were longing for the war to end.

There is virtually no record of the 137th Staffordshire Brigade during June, whilst the 46th (North Midland) Division held the Bethune sector under relentless shelling, including gas. Air raids were frequent and dangerous - a nasty side affect of these were our own anti-aircraft shell fragments. Daylight patrols took prisoners who were interrogated eagerly, as it was thought the Germans were thinking of withdrawing. Though the 137th Staffordshire Brigade had a counter-attack role out of the trenches, they were not used for this, but instead, completed much useful salvage work. Nearing the end of August the enemy started to straighten their line as a prelude to retiring, but any inquisitiveness by the British was immediately punished with accurate shelling.

The 46th (North Midland) Division left the Bethune sector it had held so well and for so long on 5th September, for intense training behind the line with the emphasis on attack. There was great optimism that the enemy's power was at last to be extinguished, and after its long period of static warfare, the Division hoped to be in on the "kill". On the 19th, the 137th Staffordshire Brigade, with reduced baggage, moved through the ruins of the Somme valley towards the St. Quentin Canal, the Division having been transferred to the 9th Corps. The 46th (North Midland) Division was ordered to assault the enemy across the St. Quentin Canal which consisted of a cutting about forty feet deep with steeply banked sides. The canal was brick lined and the water was about 8 feet deep. Enemy outposts were forward of this, but the bulk of the German defences were in considerable depth behind. Eighteen months of un-molested hard work and German ingenuity, had made them virtually impregnable. However, one weakness was that a bridge at Requeval had been left intact along with several foot bridges to serve the enemy front

A contemporary British Brodie steel helmet and helmet cover, carrying a badge identifying it as belonging to the 1/6th South Staffs.

46th North Midland Divisional Christmas cards, 1917 and 1918.

line. The German defences were so strong in fact, our Higher Command regarded their attack as a forlorn hope, and the object was mainly to pin down enemy reserves. An American division was meant to break through to the left, where the canal went through a tunnel, but it was bloodily repulsed.

The plan was for the 137th Staffordshire Brigade to break into the position and for the other two brigades of the 46th (North Midland) Division to follow up, exploiting their success. The 137th Stafford Brigade were to attack with its three battalions in line, the South Staffs right and centre, and the 1/6th North Staffs (the 1/5th had been broken up when all brigades were reduced to three battalions earlier in the year) on the left. The vital Riqueval Bridge lay in the North sector.

Rehearsals had included the use of light bridges, collapsible boats and lifebelts to the grim amusement of the troops. However, when they discovered that the boats and lifebelts had to be carried by the already overburdened troops, their amusement abruptly ceased. The attack started on 23rd September when the 138th (Lincoln and Leicester) Brigade, after desperate fighting, partially took Pontruet, a village stronghold a mile west of the canal. At this point the 1/6th South Staffs received casualties from enemy artillery retaliation. At dusk on the 27th, the 137th Staffordshire Brigade relieved the 138th, who had cleared enemy positions west of the canal; British artillery had accumulated in such numbers that before the attack the normal camouflage and cover had to be ignored.

During the 28th the 1/5th South Staffs, in the line north west of Bellenglise, were strongly counter-attacked by the enemy in an attempt to retrieve the captured trenches. The outpost companies were forced back and accurate enemy shelling held up ammunition replenishment and the arrival of reinforcements. The 1/5th South Staffs lost half their strength.

Zero hour was 5.50am on September 29th, and as on March 21st 1918, the 137th Brigade attacked with the 1/6th North Staffs left, 1/5th South Staffs centre and the 1/6th South Staffs right. From the Diary of the 1/5th South Staffs we learn that the initial assault started in clear weather. This deteriorated at once into dense fog. As the men got closer to the enemy positions, their own barrage crept forward with deadly accuracy. It was far worse than the normal smoke and mist of the battlefield. The forward German defences were soon overrun, but as the leading company of North Staffs moved down a ravine towards the vital bridge, they were held up by an enemy machine gun. The Company Commander, Captain Charlton, led forward a party who captured the German machine gun and then rushed the bridge.

As they approached, some Germans emerged from their dug-outs as the barrage crept forward past their positions and ran to fire the charges, but the Staffords got there first, the enemy were shot and the charges thrown into the canal.

Then the whole Company stormed across and had soon taken 130 prisoners including an enemy battalion commander. For once the deep, strong concrete dug-outs were a real disadvantage to the enemy, for although they saved many during the preliminary bombardments and barrage, before the occupants could emerge and fight they were bombed and killed or forced to surrender. In fact large parties yielded to one or two men. Meanwhile, the rest of the 1/6th North Staffs were across the canal and on top of the defenders of the main position before they realised what was happening. Having reorganised, the Staffords swept on to their final objective, well within the planned time limit. By 8.30am forward HQs were over the canal, and at 10 am, the supporting Brigade was passing through the 137th. Many enemy prisoners, who were waiting to go back, were killed by their own shells. The Germans had suffered very heavily with over 4,000 prisoners taken in addition to the large number killed and wounded. Some fifty guns, several mortars and many machine guns were captured. Numerous messages of congratulations to the Division contain special mention of the 137th Staffordshire Brigade.

The 137th Staffordshire Brigade had advanced 2,000 yards, crossed a major obstacle and broken through defences as strong as any on the Western Front, in two and a half hours. It was one of the most brilliant performances by British infantry in the whole war. The War Diary of the 1/6th South Staffs describes its most famous day briefly thus: *"29th. At 5.30 a.m. under a heavy artillery and machine-gun barrage the Battalion as part of the 137th Brigade crossed the ST QUENTIN CANAL and captured the HINDENBURG LINE and the village of BELLENGLISE"*. It is interesting to note this success was gained only two miles north of where the 1st Battalion of the North Staffs was overwhelmed by the enemy six months before. The territorials had truly avenged their regular comrades.

Amongst the heroes of the St. Quentin Canal crossing was a stretcher bearer, Lance-Corporal Coltman, who received a bar to his DCM for bringing in wounded under fire. He already had an MM. and bar and three weeks later at Sequehart, during the final advance, he was to earn the Victoria Cross, and survive!

It was important to follow up the enemy and on 3rd October an attack was ordered on their former reserve line between Montbrehain and Sequehart, five miles east of the crossing. All three battalions were forward, each with two companies in the leading wave, and assembled on

A photo of Brigadier Campbell VC thanking his units of the 137th Staffordshire Brigade from a very damaged Requeval Bridge over the canal - showing what a very formidable obstacle it was.

unknown ground in pitch darkness. There was some severe shelling and the 1/5th South Staffs were forced to change position. Despite this the Brigade advanced and had taken its objective by 10am against strong opposition. The Brigade to the left however failed to capture Montbrehain, and the right hand division, after occupying Sequehart, were forced out, but successfully counter-attacked later. Had the attack penetrated the enemy's trench system, the High Command's intention was for the British Cavalry to break through.

But there was delay, causing the 137th Staffordshire Brigade to suffer ever-increasing pressure and, after repelling several fierce attacks, they were driven back. Still later the same day, the 139th (Sherwood Forester) Brigade advanced in support and at night a dismounted cavalry regiment also arrived adding to the congestion and confusion in the overcrowded trenches. Outposts sent forward by the 1/6th South Staffs were forced to withdraw under intense enfilade fire of machine guns, that also probably caused the cancellation of the attack scheduled for the next day, the 4th.

The Brigade were relieved that night, but the rest was short lived as the enemy retreated quickly in front of the relentless pursuit. All was quiet as the 137th Staffordshire Brigade passed the scene of the fierce fighting of the 3rd and 4th. On the 9th it was learned the Germans had evacuated Fresnoy and were retiring north east, and Fresnoy was found intact, without booby traps. Speed was now more important to them than destruction and looting.

The Germans made another stand at Riquerval Wood, east of Bohain. The 46th (North Midland) Division, on the extreme right of the British line, attacked in cooperation with a French Division. On the 12th, the 1/5th South Staffs led the assault, supported by the 1/6th, but were unable to capture the wood in face of heavy artillery fire and deadly machine gun fire. On their return they had in turn to beat off enemy attacks. But it had helped the French to secure their objective, its commander paying generous tribute to the Brigade. The heavy casualties of the 1/5th South Staffs near to the war's end was tragic. The number of 1/6th casualties is unknown but was considerably less.

Another attack with the French, on the 17th, was much easier and they quickly took their objectives, possibly as the enemy had in the main retired, and only covering troops were engaged. The 137th Staffordshire Brigade made no further advance until November. It may be appropriate here, to refer to the lies spread by the Nazis in the 1939-1945 War that their army had not been defeated in 1918, but let down by the civilians and politicians. In fact the enemy had been beaten in the field and was in retreat everywhere, broken and with resistance disintegrating, though shelling was still dangerous. The German army was certainly in no condition to continue fighting even if the desire had been there. Many formations and units had mutinied and there was nothing to prevent the Allies occupying the whole of Germany as Foch wished - had his advice been taken, the Second World War might have been avoided.

Germany's allies, too were defeated. The Turks had been overwhelmed in Palestine, the Bulgarians in the Balkans, and the Austrians in Italy. Under these circumstances the war ended almost as suddenly as it had begun. The German Emperor and the Crown Prince fled into Holland, and the new Government demanded an armistice.

In the meantime the next objective for the 46th (North Midland) Division was Avesnes, thirty miles from the last engagement. There was no doubt the Germans were on the run. As the Staffords marched east they received great enthusiasm from French civilians, who had endured the enemy occupation. However, supplies could not keep up with the speed of the advance, and by 5th of November the Brigade were on short rations. On their approach to Avesnes on the 9th, the 46th (North Midland) Division suffered its last shelling of the war . The next day it was learnt the armistice was to be the 11th. On November 11th, 1918, the Armistice was signed. Fighting ceased on all fronts at 11am.

The 46th (North Midland) Division had been away from England for over three years and eight months. They had come out early in 1915, an unknown division of territorials, but, by their splendid prowess during these three years, they had made the 46th (North Midland) Division one of the most famous divisions of the British Army.

Bibliography

History of the South Staffordshire Regiment (1705-1923) J. P. Jones. Whitehead Bros. Wolverhampton, 1923. .

History of the South Staffordshire Regiment Col. W. L. Vale. Gale and Polden, Aldershot, 1969.

The North Staffordshire Regiment Col. H.C.B. Cook, OBE. Famous Regiments Series, Leo Cooper.

The Volunteer Artillery (1859-1908) Norman E. H. Litchfield and Ray Westlake. Sherwood Press, Nottingham, 1982.

Over There -A Commemorative History of The Old Leek Battery (1908-1919) J.E. Blore and J.R. Sherratt. 1991.

Norton's Terrier (Draft Copy) Andrew Thornton, 1996.

The Etruria Artillery - An Artillery Volunteer Corps (1859-1880) S.S. Corkerry. The Victorian Military Society, 1988.

The Uniforms of the British Yeomanry Force 1794-1914. No 15: Staffordshire Yeomanry R. J. Smith and C. R. Coogan. Robert Ogilby Trust with the Army Museums Ogilby Trust, 1993.

History of the 1st and 2nd Battalions The North Staffordshire Regiment (The Prince of Wales's) 1914-1923
Hughes & Harber Ltd., Longton, Staffordshire, 1932.

Historical Records of the 3rd King's Own Staffordshire Militia Capt. C.C.W. Troughton. A.C. Lomax, Lichfield, 1894.

A History of the 5th North Staffords, 1914-19 Lieut. W. Meakin. Hughes & Harber, Longton, Staffordshire, 1920.

War History of the 6th Battalion The South Staffordshire Regiment (T.F.) A Committee of Officers. Heinemann, 1924.

The Unbreakable Coil Major A.L.K. Anderson. Whitehead Bros, Wolverhampton.

Breaking the Hindenburg Line (Story of the 46th (North Midland) Div.) R. E. Priestley MC. T. Fisher Unwin, 1919.

Memoirs of the Services of the 64th Regiment (Second Staffordshire) (1758-1881) H.G. Purdon 64th Regt. WH Allen.

Records of the Queen's Own Royal Yeomanry P.C.G. Webster. Thomas George Lomax, Lichfield, 1870.

The Staffords 1881-1978 G. Rosignoli and Capt. C. J Whitehouse. Rosignoli, Farnham, 1978.

The Staffords: Tying the Knot. A History of the Staffordshire Regiment from 1705 to 1991 told in a series of original illustrations by Rob Chapman, Flintlock Publishing, 10 Westbourne Road, Walsall, WS4 2JA.

A Short History of The Staffordshire Regiment (The Prince of Wales's) Col W.L. Vale. Whitehead Bros.

1914-1915 Leek & District Sailors & Soldiers Roll of Honour Hariette Smith, Leek - David Morris & Co, Leek.

The Zulu War and the 80th Regiment of Foot Robert Hope - Churnet Valley, Leek. 1995.

Colours, Battle Honours and Medals of a Staffordshire Regiment: 80th Regt of Foot Robert Hope, Churnet Valley.

Collecting Volunteer Militaria R. J. Wyatt. David & Charles.

Weapons & Equipment of the Victorian Soldier Donald Featherstone. Blandford, 1978.

Dress Regulations For The Army 1900 Originally published by HM SO in 1900, reprinted by David & Charles, 1970.

Head Dress of the British Heavy Cavalry - Dragoon Guards, Household and Yeomanry Cavalry 1842-1934
David J.J. Rowe. Schiffer, USA.

Worth Saving: The Staffordshire Regiment's fight for survival. Bruce George MP & Nick Ryan. Smith Settle 1996

Shoulder belt plates 5th Staffordshire Rifle Volunteers, Glengarry badge and waist belt clasp.

LEFT: Colonel Bromley-Davenport's Albert Pattern helmet, with post 1860's white plume - prior to this the plume would have been black.

ABOVE: An officer's bell top shako of the Staffordshire Yeomanry Cavalry, circa 1829-1844

Staffordshire Yeomanry cap badge, with Queen's Crown, as adopted for wear by the Regiment's ordinary ranks. This particular badge was worn officially until the end of the Second World War.

An 80th officer's shoulder belt plate c. 1810.

A Victorian South Staffords officer's belt buckle.

Sutlej Campaign Medal of William Reeves who died of wounds 04/02/1846, so no Sobraon bar.

Sutlej Campaign medal of John Ross who received the Ferozeshuhur and Sobraon bar.

India General Service Campaign medal of Sergeant D. King with the Pegu bar.

The India General Service Campaign medal of 396 T Chatfield with the Bhootan bar.

The Perak and South Africa (Zulu War) Campaign Medal pair of 108 Pte M. Arthurs (This Perak bar of the India General Service Campaign Medal, was one of only 300 to the 80th Regiment)

LEFT: An other ranks Glengarry badge of the 80th.

RIGHT: Glengarry badge of the 98th Foot.

BELOW: Punjab campaign medal awarded to "Wm. Charles 98th Foot"

China 1842 campaign medal awarded to "John Bannister 98th Regiment Foot".

India General Service Medal with the North West Frontier bar, awarded to Lieut T. F. Swinford of HM's 98th Foot (but attached to the 5th Punjab Infantry for this action).

An officer's blue cloth, home service helmet plate of the 64th Foot c1878-1881.

Various 80th officer's coatee and other ranks numbered buttons.

Numbered buttons of the 98th Foot including mess waiters.

The Egypt and Khedive's
Star of Pte. A. Wall.

An officer's and an other
ranks, 1st Volunteer
Battalion, Glengarry badge,
and a 2nd Volunteer
Battalion other ranks
Glengarry badge.

Bottom: An officer's sword
belt buckle.

A Victorian Regular and 1st Volunteer Battalion cap badge, along with a Victorian 'sweet heart' brooch and Boer War period bordered, brass shoulder title.

RIGHT:
Victorian 1st Volunteer Battalion, 2nd V.B., 3rd V.B. and officer's 1st V.B. Glengarry badges.

Pte A. Rowbotham's Boer War Tribute Medal group.

A group of other ranks regular and volunteer, Queen's and King's crown blue cloth helmet plates.

Pte A. Rowbotham's Boer War Tribute Medal group.